my revision notes

WJEC GCSE
HISTORY
Route B

R. Paul Evans

HODDER
EDUCATION
AN HACHETTE UK COMPANY

For Janet, in grateful appreciation of her continued encouragement and support.

Text acknowledgements

Thanks to WJEC for permission to reproduce exam question on **pages 54, 107 and 130.**

p.39 *The Welsh Academy Encyclopaedia of Wales*, co-edited by John Davies, Nigel Jenkins, Menna Baines, Peredur Lynch, (University of Wales Press, Cardiff, 2008), pg.781–82; **p.42** Mike Huggins, *British Newsreels, Soccer and Popular Culture 1918–39* (2007). Quoted in *Developments in Sport, Leisure & Tourism during the 20th century* by Phil Star, (CAA publications, Aberystwyth University, 2012), pg.23, source G; **p.46** Reproduced in *Developments in Sport, Leisure & Tourism during the 20th century* by Phil Star, (CAA publications, Aberystwyth University, 2012), pg.33, source F; **p.63** Quoted from *Travel & Tourism by Christine King*, Andy Kerr, Malcolm Jefferies, (Heinemann, 2006), pg. 19; **p.100** Quoted from 'Edexcel Crime and Punishment through time' by Donald Cumming and Joanne Philpott (Hodder Education, 2011).

Photo acknowledgements

Cover © DNY59/istockphoto.com; **page 20** © Solo Syndication/Associated Newspapers Ltd.; **page 61** © The Imperial Hotel, Llandudno; **page 93** © Mary Evans Picture Library/Alamy; **page 100** © Mary Evans Picture Library/Alamy; **page 107** © INTERFOTO/Alamy; **page 130** © Mansell/Time Life Pictures/Getty Images.

Every effort has been made to trace all copyright holders, but if any have been inadvertently overlooked the Publishers will be pleased to make the necessary arrangements at the first opportunity.

Although every effort has been made to ensure that website addresses are correct at time of going to press, Hodder Education cannot be held responsible for the content of any website mentioned in this book. It is sometimes possible to find a relocated web page by typing in the address of the home page for a website in the URL window of your browser.

Hachette UK's policy is to use papers that are natural, renewable and recyclable products and made from wood grown in sustainable forests. The logging and manufacturing processes are expected to conform to the environmental regulations of the country of origin.

Orders: please contact Bookpoint Ltd, 130 Milton Park, Abingdon, Oxon OX14 4SB. Telephone: +44 (0)1235 827720. Fax: +44 (0)1235 400454. Lines are open 9.00a.m.–5.00p.m., Monday to Saturday, with a 24-hour message answering service. Visit our website at www.hoddereducation.co.uk.

© R. Paul Evans 2014
First published in 2014 by
Hodder Education,
an Hachette UK company
338 Euston Road
London NW1 3BH

Impression number   10 9 8 7 6 5 4 3 2 1

Year   2018 2017 2016 2015 2014

Typeset in Datapage (India) Pvt. Ltd.
Artwork by Datapage (India) Pvt. Ltd.
Printed and bound in India

A catalogue record for this title is available from the British Library

ISBN 978 1 444 19778 5

Get the most from this book

This book will help you revise for the WJEC GCSE History Route B specification, which can be downloaded from the WJEC website www.wjec.co.uk. Follow the links to GCSE History specification B.

This book covers the Depth Study **Germany in transition, c.1929–1947,** the Thematic Study **Developments in sport, leisure and tourism in Wales and England, 1900 to the present day**, and the Development Studies **Changes in crime and punishment in Wales and England, c.1530 to the present day** and **Changes in health and medicine, c.1345 to the present day**.

You can use the revision planner on pages 4 and 5 to plan your revision, topic by topic. Tick each box when you have:

1. revised and understood a topic
2. answered the exam practice questions
3. checked your answers online.

You can also keep track of your revision by ticking off each topic heading throughout the book. Be a scribbler, make notes as you learn. You will need an exercise book for most of the revision tasks, but you can also write in this book.

✓ Tick to track your progress

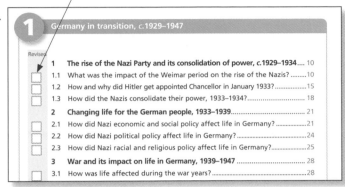

Revision tasks

Use these tasks to make sure that you have understood every topic and to help you think about what you are revising. If you do the tasks you will have to use the information in the book. If you use the information you will remember it better. The more you use it the better you will remember it.

Exam practice

Sample exam questions are provided for each topic. Use them to consolidate your revision and practise your exam skills.

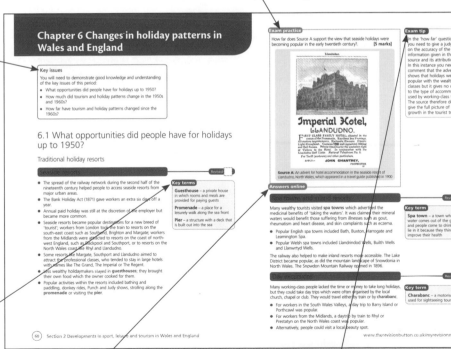

Key issues

Key issues from the specification are listed on the first page of each chapter. You need to have a good knowledge and understanding of these issues.

Key terms

Key terms are highlighted the first time they appear, with an explanation nearby in the margin.

Go online

Go online to check your answers to the exam questions, and try out the quick quizzes at **www.therevisionbutton. co.uk/myrevisionnotes.**

Exam tip

Throughout the book there are exam tips that explain how you can boost your final grade.

Contents and revision planner

Introduction

How to revise

There is no single way to revise, but there are some good ideas on these pages.

1. Make a revision timetable

For a subject like history, which involves learning large amounts of factual detail, it is essential that you construct a 'revision plan':

- **Start early** – you should start by looking at the dates of your exams and work backwards to the first date you intend to start revising, probably 6 to 8 weeks before your exam.

- **Be realistic** – work out a realistic plan to complete your revision; don't try to do too much. Remember you have to fit in your history revision alongside your other GCSE subjects. Plan to include rest breaks.

- **Revise regularly** – regular, short spells of 40 minutes are better than panicky six-hour slogs until 2a.m.

- **Plan your time carefully** – give more revision time to topic areas you find difficult and spend longer on the sections you feel less confident about.

- **Track your progress** – keep to your timetable, and use the revision planner on pages 4 and 5 to tick off each topic as you complete it. Give yourself targets and reward yourself when you have achieved them.

2. Revise actively

Different people revise in different ways and you will have to find the methods which best suit your learning style. Here are some techniques which students have used to help them revise:

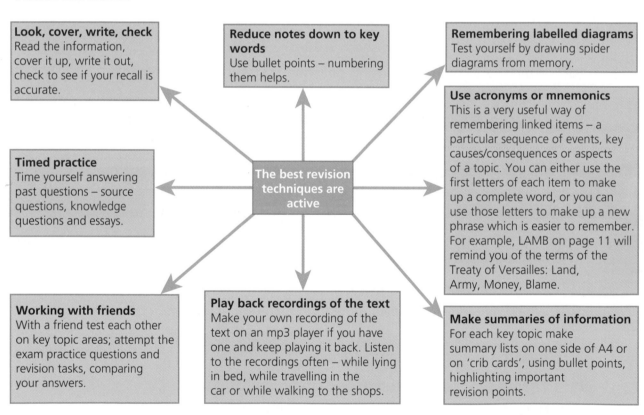

Look, cover, write, check
Read the information, cover it up, write it out, check to see if your recall is accurate.

Reduce notes down to key words
Use bullet points – numbering them helps.

Remembering labelled diagrams
Test yourself by drawing spider diagrams from memory.

Use acronyms or mnemonics
This is a very useful way of remembering linked items – a particular sequence of events, key causes/consequences or aspects of a topic. You can either use the first letters of each item to make up a complete word, or you can use those letters to make up a new phrase which is easier to remember. For example, LAMB on page 11 will remind you of the terms of the Treaty of Versailles: Land, Army, Money, Blame.

Timed practice
Time yourself answering past questions – source questions, knowledge questions and essays.

The best revision techniques are active

Working with friends
With a friend test each other on key topic areas; attempt the exam practice questions and revision tasks, comparing your answers.

Play back recordings of the text
Make your own recording of the text on an mp3 player if you have one and keep playing it back. Listen to the recordings often – while lying in bed, while travelling in the car or while walking to the shops.

Make summaries of information
For each key topic make summary lists on one side of A4 or on 'crib cards', using bullet points, highlighting important revision points.

How to prepare for the exam

1. Decode the exam question

To perform well in the exam, you will have to answer the questions correctly. To understand what the question is asking, look for the key command words which will tell you the type of answer you should write. Common command words and their meanings are:

- **Explain** Provide a number of reasons, showing how or why each contributed to the event named in the question.
- **Describe** Provide specific factual detail on the key issue named in the question.
- **How important/successful/How far......** Provide a judgement on the named event/person supported by reasons, explanations and evidence.

2. Look at the mark schemes

All your answers on the exam paper will be marked by using a level of response mark scheme. In the low tariff questions (2–4 marks) there will normally be two levels, for the medium tariff questions (5–7 marks) there will be three levels and for the higher tariff questions (8–10 marks) there will be four levels. The more detailed, informed and well reasoned your answer is, the higher up the level of responses you will advance.

A typical level of response mark scheme will look like this:

Level 1: Generalised points, not fully focused on the topic area being examined; the general points will not be supported by accurate or relevant factual details or examples.

Answers will be very simplistic and contain little factual support.

Level 2: A number of relevant points with some focus on the question; these points will be supported by accurate factual detail, although the range might be narrow or some points might not be fully developed.

Answers will display good focus, will be supported with relevant detail and demonstrate an argument which goes some way to answering the question.

Level 3: A range of relevant points which clearly address the question and show understanding of the most important factors involved; a clear explanation which is well structured and supported by detailed and accurate factual information.

Answers will be thorough and detailed; they will clearly engage with the question and provide a balanced and reasoned argument that reaches a well-supported judgement.

Guide to the WJEC GCSE History examination

You will be examined on Units 1, 2 and 3. Unit 4 is the controlled assessment unit, which will be completed in class under the supervision of your history teacher and is not covered in this book.

How the WJEC GCSE History specification (Route B) is organised

Unit	Unit type	Examination	Mark weighting
Unit 1	A Study in Depth	1 hour 15 minutes	50 marks
Unit 2	A Thematic Study	1 hour 15 minutes	50 marks
Unit 3	A Development Study	1 hour 15 minutes	50 marks
Unit 4	Controlled Assessment – an investigation into an issue of historical debate or controversy	No exam – completed in class under controlled conditions	50 marks

This book covers the Depth Study relating to **Germany**, a Thematic Study relating to **Sport, Leisure and Tourism**, and two Development Studies relating to **Changes in Crime and Punishment**, and **Changes in Health and Medicine**.

Units 1 and 2

The examinations for Units 1 and 2 will test your knowledge and understanding of the key developments in each of the three sections for the Depth Study or Thematic Study you have studied. You will have to answer three sections, each testing particular skills.

Section A – Source evaluation

You must answer all the questions in this section.

- **Question 1(a)** is worth **2 marks** and asks you to select information from a visual source:

  a) What does Source A show you about ...?

  – Pick out at least two details from the source that are relevant to the question.

  – Make use of the information in the caption.

  – Do not bring in any other factual knowledge as this will not gain you any extra marks.

- **Question 1(b)** is worth **4 marks** and asks you to explain a source and place it in its historical context by using your own knowledge:

  b) Use the information in Source B and your own knowledge to explain why ...

  – Pick out at least two details from the source and explain them in your own words.

  – You must demonstrate your knowledge of this topic by providing at least one additional factor that is not mentioned in the source.

- **Question 1(c)** is worth **5 marks** and asks you to analyse a source and make a judgement on the extent to which it supports a view:

  c) How far does Source C support the view that ...?

  – Pick out a range of relevant details from both the source and the caption, explaining them in your own words.

  – Bring in your own knowledge to expand on the details from the source and to provide additional material.

  – Give a reasoned judgement which addresses the question.

- **Question 1(d)** is worth **6 marks** and asks you to decide how useful a source is to a historian:

  d) How useful is Source D to a historian studying ...?

  – Look at the content, origin and purpose of the source:

    ○ Content – What does the source say?

    ○ Origin –Who said it? When did they say it?

    ○ Purpose – Why was it said? Who was it said to and why? Is it biased?

  – Make reference to the usefulness of the source to the historian – what are the limitations? Has any important information been left out?

  – Remember that a source can be useful even if it is not reliable; what might it be useful for?

- **Question 1(e)** is worth **8 marks** and requires you to cross-reference two sources to look at their differing views about a historical issue:

  e) Why do Sources E and F have different views about ...?

  – You must comment on both sources, in each case making reference to the content and the author.

  – Think about how the sources fit into your knowledge of this period; is there anything missing?

  – Explain why the sources have different views.

Section B – Knowledge and understanding

You must answer all the questions in this section.

- **Question 2(a)** is worth **4 marks** and tests your knowledge and understanding of key features:

  a) Describe the ...

  – You must describe at least two key features.

  – Only include information that is directly relevant.

  – Be specific; avoid generalised comments.

- **Question 2(b)** is worth **5 marks** and asks you to explain why something happened during this period.

  b) Explain why ...

  – Give a variety of well-explained reasons.

  – Give specific details such as names, dates, events, organisations and activities.

  – Always support your statements with examples.

  – Make sure the information you include is directly relevant and answers the question.

- **Question 2(c)** is worth **6 marks** and asks you to evaluate why a person, event or development was significant or important.

  c) How important was ...?

  – Evaluate the importance or significance of the named individual, event or issue.

  – You must provide a judgement, giving specific reasons to support your answer.

Section C – Essay writing

You must answer the essay question which is set.

- **Question 3** is worth **10 marks**, with **3 additional marks** for Spelling, Punctuation and Grammar (SPaG).

    Did ... succeed in ...?

    Was ... the most important reason/development ...?

    – You need to develop a two-sided answer: discuss the key feature mentioned in the question and follow this by discussing other important factors.

    – Avoid generalised comments: give specific detail and ensure that you cover a range of factors/key issues.

    – Remember the rules of essay writing: ensure your answer has an introduction, several paragraphs of discussion and a reasoned conclusion which provides a judgement on the question set.

Unit 3

Section A – Knowledge and understanding

Three questions will appear in Section A – you have to answer **two.** They will each follow the same format of questions:

- **Question 1(a)** is worth **2 marks** and asks you to explain the message(s) from a visual source:

    a) What does Source A show you about ...?

    – Pick out at least two details from the source that are relevant to the question.

    – Make use of the information in the caption.

    – Do not bring in any other factual knowledge as this will not gain you any extra marks.

- **Question 1(b)** is worth **4 marks** and tests your knowledge and understanding of key features:

    b) Describe the ...

    – You must describe at least two key features.

    – Only include information that is directly relevant.

    – Be specific; avoid generalised comments.

- **Question 1(c)** is worth **6 marks** and you are asked to identify change or lack of change, using your own knowledge to place each source into context:

    c) Use Sources B and C and your own knowledge to explain why ... had changed.

    – You must use the information in both sources and the captions attached to them, as well as your own knowledge.

    – Cross-reference the sources, pointing out what is the same or what is different.

    – Make sure you focus on the key issue of change or lack of change.

- **Question 1(d)** is worth 8 marks and asks you to evaluate importance or success.

    d) How important/successful was ...?

    – Evaluate the importance, significance or success of the named individual, event or issue.

    – You must provide a judgement, giving specific reasons to support your answer.

Section B – Essay writing

You will be required to answer **one** essay question from a choice of three: questions 4, 5 or 6.

How far had ... changed/improved between ... and the present day?

How important/successful has .... been between ... and the present day?

Have changes in ... always improved from ... and the present day?

- You must include information from across the whole time period, **either** 1530 to the present day **or** 1345 to the present day. Do not spend too long on one time period e.g. the nineteenth century.

- You must try to cover at least **three** timeframes to make sure you discuss as much of the period as possible; e.g. the sixteenth and seventeenth centuries, the eighteenth and nineteenth centuries, and the twentieth century up to the present day.

- You must show how things have changed or stayed the same, remembering that some time periods will show a faster pace of change than others – make sure you explain the reasons for this.

- Remember the rules of essay writing: ensure your answer has an introduction, several paragraphs of discussion and a reasoned conclusion which provides a judgement on the question set.

Chapter 1 The rise of the Nazi Party and its consolidation of power, *c.*1929–1934

Key issues

You will need to demonstrate good knowledge and understanding of the key issues of this period:

- What was the impact of the Weimar period on the rise of the Nazis?
- How and why did Hitler get appointed Chancellor in January 1933?
- How did the Nazis consolidate their power, 1933–1934?

1.1 What was the impact of the Weimar period on the rise of the Nazis?

The political and economic problems of Weimar

The Weimar Republic
Revised ☐

By the autumn of 1918 the German army was on the point of collapse. On 9 November the Kaiser abdicated and fled to the Netherlands. Germany became a **republic** and on 11 November the provisional government agreed to an armistice which brought Germany's fighting in the First World War to an end. Not all Germans welcomed the new republic and Berlin faced armed unrest from both left-wing and right-wing extremist groups. For this reason the newly elected Constituent Assembly, which met for the first time in January 1919, did so in the town of Weimar in southern Germany. This town gave its name to the **Weimar Republic**.

The Weimar Republic lasted from 1919 to 1933. During that time it was ruled by two Presidents – Friedrich Ebert (1918–25) and Paul von Hindenburg (1925–34). They often battled to keep weak and unstable governments in office. The Republic faced many weaknesses.

Key terms

Republic – a government in which supreme power is exercised by representatives elected by the people

Weimar Republic – following the abdication of the Kaiser in November 1918, Germany became a republic. It is named after the town of Weimar where the temporary government met to write a new constitution

The weaknesses of the Weimar Constitution
Revised ☐

Appointment of Chancellor – the Chancellor was appointed by the President and was meant to be the leader of the largest party. After 1930 President Hindenburg appointed chancellors who did not lead the largest party and allowed them to rule using Article 48.

System of voting – use of **proportional representation** (PR) to elect members of the **Reichstag**.

Frequent changes of government –during the Republic there were nine elections, two each in the years 1923 and 1932. This resulted in weak and often unstable government.

Weaknesses of the Weimar Republic

Coalition government – the use of PR meant that parties obtained seats in the Reichstag in direct proportion to the total number of votes cast for them. This made it difficult for any one party to achieve an overall majority and resulted in coalition government.

Power of the President – during times of crisis the President could use Article 48 of the constitution to declare a 'state of emergency' and rule by Presidential decree. This was dangerous as it meant that laws could be passed without the approval of the Reichstag.

Until the appointment of Hitler most Chancellors came from moderate parties, yet they ruled over Reichstags which included extreme parties such as the Communists and Nazis, both of whom wanted to destroy the Republic.

Revision task

Copy and complete the following table to show how each factor helped to weaken the Weimar Republic.

	How this factor helped to weaken the Weimar Republic
Proportional representation	
Coalition government	
Article 48	

Key terms

Proportional representation – system where the number of votes won in an election directly determines the number of seats in parliament

Reichstag – the German parliament

Coalition government – a government made up of two or more political parties

The Treaty of Versailles, 1919

Revised

The new German government had no choice but to sign the Treaty of Versailles on 28 June 1919 which formally punished Germany for its involvement in the First World War. The majority of Germans were horrified by the terms and viewed the treaty as a great humiliation.

The treaty contained 440 clauses. The main terms were:

- **territorial terms:** Germany lost 13 per cent of its **land**, 6 million citizens and all her colonial possessions; Germany was forbidden to unite with Austria, Alsace-Lorraine was given to France; East Prussia was to be cut off from the rest of Germany by the Polish corridor; the Saarland was to be administered by the League of Nations

- **military terms:** the German **army** was limited to 100,000 men; it was forbidden to possess any tanks, heavy guns, aircraft or submarines; its navy was limited to ships of less than 10,000 tons; the Rhineland was to be demilitarised

- **financial terms:** under Clause 231 (War Guilt) Germany had to accept full responsibility for having caused the war and agree to pay **money** as reparations for the damage caused (a figure of £6600 million was fixed in 1921)

- **political terms:** Germany was forbidden to join the newly created League of Nations. Germany also had to accept **blame** for causing the war.

Key term

Reparations – war damages to be paid by Germany

Exam tip

For your exam you need to remember the key terms in the treaty. To remember these, use the acronym **LAMB**.

LAND

ARMY

MONEY

BLAME

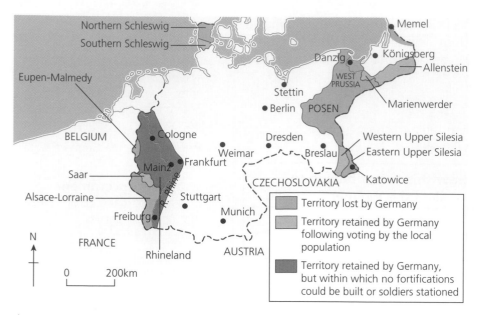

↑ Territorial terms of the Treaty of Versailles

The shame and humiliation of the Treaty, and the fact that the Germans were not allowed any role in negotiating the terms, gave ammunition to the opponents of Weimar, especially the extreme parties.

Exam practice

Source A: An extract from the German newspaper *Deutsche Zeitung*, June 1919

'Today in the Hall of Mirrors the disgraceful treaty is being signed. Do not forget it. The German people will with unceasing [constant] labour press forward to reconquer the place among nations to which is it entitled. Then will come vengeance [revenge] for the shame of 1919.'

Use the information in Source A and your own knowledge to explain why many German people disliked the Treaty of Versailles. **[4 marks]**

Answers online

Exam tip

This type of question requires you to do two things – discuss what is said in the source and add additional points from your own knowledge of this topic. In this instance the source talks about the shame and humiliation felt by many Germans and you could add to it by writing about the military, territorial or financial terms of the Treaty.

The early development of the Nazi Party

The origins of the Nazi Party

Revised

In 1919 Anton Drexler founded the German Workers Party (*Deutsche Arbeiter Partei,* DAP) in Munich, Bavaria. It was a right-wing, nationalistic party which stressed the ideal of a pure German people. While working for the army intelligence unit, Adolf Hitler attended a meeting in September 1919. He liked what he heard and was invited to join. His organisational ability was quickly recognised and in 1920 he was put in charge of the party's propaganda machine. In February 1920 Hitler and Drexler wrote the party's 'Twenty-Five Point Programme', which became its political manifesto. In July 1921 Hitler replaced Drexler as leader and he changed the name of the party to National Socialist German Workers Party (NSDAP). He adopted the title *Führer* (leader), developed a party symbol, the swastika, and introduced the raised arm salute.

Early growth of the Nazi Party

Revised

Party membership increased from 1100 members in June 1920 to 55,000 in November 1923. In 1921 Hitler set up the *Sturmabteilung* (SA) which was led by Ernst Roehm. Often referred to as the 'Brownshirts' because of the colour of their uniform or the 'Stormtroopers', this armed group of mostly ex-military men were charged with protecting Nazi speakers from attacks by rival political groups.

The political atmosphere in the early years of Weimar was one of chaos and disruption.

- In 1919 there was an attempted Communist revolution (the Spartacist Rising) in Berlin and in 1920 there was an attempted right-wing takeover (the Kapp **Putsch**).
- When Germany failed to make the second reparation payment in 1923, French and Belgium troops marched into the Ruhr to take control of the coalfields.
- In protest, German workers were encouraged to go on strike, the government supplying their wages. The government had to print more and more money and the result was the collapse of the currency and raging inflation.
- By November 1923 Germany was plagued by hyperinflation.

In this atmosphere of political and financial chaos, Hitler thought the time was right for the Nazi Party to seize power, first in the Bavarian state capital in Munich, followed by a march on Berlin.

> **Key term**
>
> **Putsch** – a political uprising

> **Revision task**
>
> Construct a timeline to show the key events in the history of the Nazi Party between January 1919 and November 1923.

The Munich Putsch, 8–9 November 1923

Revised

On the evening of 8 November 1923, Hitler and 600 SA men burst into a public meeting held in the Burgerbrau beer hall in Munich which was being addressed by Gustav von Kahr, the Bavarian Chief Minister. At gunpoint, von Kahr and the army chief von Lossow agreed to help in the planned takeover. They later informed the police and authorities of Hitler's plan.

When a Nazi force of 2000 SA men marched through Munich the following morning they were met by the police. In the clash, shots were fired in which sixteen Nazis and four policemen were killed. Hitler escaped the scene but was arrested two days later. Together with his main supporter, General Ludendorff, Hitler was put on trial and the Nazi Party was banned.

Hitler's trial started in February 1924 and lasted one month. It gave him national publicity. He criticised the '**November Criminals**', the Treaty of Versailles and the 'Jewish **Bolshevists**' who had betrayed Germany. While Ludendorff was let off, Hitler was found guilty of treason and sentenced to five years in Landsberg prison. He served only nine months.

> **Key terms**
>
> **November Criminals** – those politicians who had agreed to the signing of an armistice in November 1918
>
> **Bolshevists** or **Bolsheviks** – followers of Lenin who carried out a Communist revolution in Russia in February 1917

The importance of the Munich Putsch

Revised

Whilst in prison Hitler had time to reflect. He realised that in order to win power the Nazi Party would have to change its strategy. Instead of an armed rising, the party would have to build on recent publicity and work towards achieving a majority in the polls and be elected into office through the ballot box. He also used the time to complete his autobiography, *Mein Kampf* (*My Struggle*), which contained his political views.

> **Key term**
>
> **Anti-Semitism** – hatred and persecution of the Jews

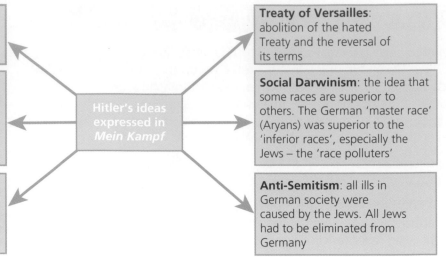

Volksgemeinschaft: the creation of a people's community

Lebensraum: obtain living space, especially in eastern Europe; create a 'Greater Germany' in which all German-speaking people would be united into one nation

Anti-Communist: socialist and communist politicians had 'stabbed Germany in the back' in 1918 by agreeing to the armistice. They were the 'November Criminals'

Hitler's ideas expressed in *Mein Kampf*

Treaty of Versailles: abolition of the hated Treaty and the reversal of its terms

Social Darwinism: the idea that some races are superior to others. The German 'master race' (Aryans) was superior to the 'inferior races', especially the Jews – the 'race polluters'

Anti-Semitism: all ills in German society were caused by the Jews. All Jews had to be eliminated from Germany

Revision task

Make a copy of the following table. Use the information in this section to complete each section, building up a picture of the importance of the Munich Putsch in the history of the Nazi Party.

	The importance of the Munich Putsch, November 1923
Aims of the Putsch	
Events of 8 November	
Events of 9 November	
The trial and sentence of the leaders of the Putsch	
Consequences of the Putsch for the Nazi Party	

Development of the Nazi Party, 1924–29

Revised ▢

On his release from prison Hitler managed to have the ban on the Nazi Party lifted and he quickly set about reorganising and re-establishing his leadership:

- He created his own bodyguard, the Schutzstaffel (SS).
- He introduced the Hitler Jugend (Hitler Youth) to attract younger members.
- He used every opportunity to attack the weaknesses of Weimar and the Nazi Party began to attract support from all classes.
- In 1925 the Party had 27,000 members and by 1928 this had increased to over 100,000.

Despite these changes, the Nazis won only twelve seats in the Reichstag in the 1928 general election, having held 32 in 1924. The lack of success was largely due to the economic recovery brought about between 1924 and 1929 by the Chancellor and later Foreign Minister, Gustav Stresemann, whose policies dissuaded people from voting for the extreme parties.

Key terms

Schutzstaffel – the SS which originally started as Hitler's private bodyguard but which grew into a powerful organisation with wide powers; they wore black uniforms

Hitler Jugend – the Hitler Youth organisation set up in 1925 to convert young Germans to Nazi ideas

Revision task

Identify three ways in which the Nazi Party developed into a more powerful political force between 1924 and 1929.

1.2 How and why did Hitler get appointed Chancellor in January 1933?

The impact of the Wall Street Crash and the Great Depression

Revised

Much of the economic recovery in Germany in the late 1920s was heavily reliant on American loans. Following the Wall Street Crash in October 1929 US banks recalled their loans. Depression hit the German economy:

Demand for consumer goods fell sharply and German firms were forced to lay off workers

↓

International trade began to contract and German exports fell rapidly

↓

Factories closed and unemployment rose sharply, reaching a peak of 6.2 million in 1932

↓

Many Germans were unable to pay their rents and found themselves homeless, living on the streets

↓

Four out of every ten German workers were without a job

↑ **The impact of US banks recalling loans in Germany**

Weimar politicians appeared to be doing too little too late and in desperation people increasingly began to turn to the extremist parties for solutions. Support for the Communists and Nazis rose sharply in the general election of September 1930.

Exam practice

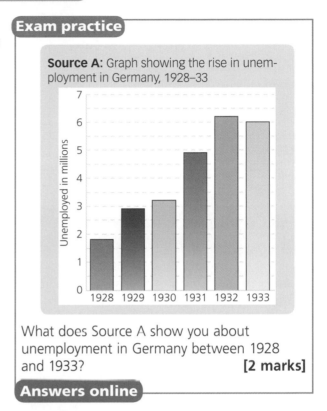

Source A: Graph showing the rise in unemployment in Germany, 1928–33

What does Source A show you about unemployment in Germany between 1928 and 1933? **[2 marks]**

Answers online

Exam tip

In this type of question you need to pick out specific detail from what you can see in the source and from the caption attached to it. In this context you need to say that the graph shows a sharp rise in unemployment, rising from under 2 million in 1928 to over 6 million in 1932. By 1933 it had begun to fall. It is important that you 'say what you see'.

The end of parliamentary democracy: the coalition of Brüning

Revised

The harsh economic climate created severe problems for the weak coalition governments of Weimar and they soon collapsed, resulting in three general elections between 1930 and 1932. In March 1930 President Hindenburg appointed Heinrich Brüning of the Centre Party as Chancellor. Brüning lacked a majority and had to rely on President Hindenburg and Article 48 to allow him to rule using Presidential Decrees. From this point on, the Reichstag was used less frequently and the use of Article 48 marked the end of parliamentary democracy in Germany.

As the Depression deepened, Brüning's government became more and more unpopular. It was forced to cut unemployment benefits and Brüning became known as the 'hunger chancellor'. In May 1932 he resigned and in the general election which followed in July the Nazis polled their highest ever vote, securing 230 seats (37 per cent) making them the largest party in the Reichstag.

Party	Elections to the Reichstag						
	May 1924	Dec 1924	May 1928	Sept 1930	July 1932	Nov 1932	March 1933
Social Democrats	100	131	152	143	133	121	120
Centre Party	65	69	61	68	75	70	73
People's Party	44	51	45	30	7	11	2
Democrats	28	32	25	14	4	2	5
Communists	62	45	54	77	89	100	81
Nationalists	106	103	79	41	40	51	53
Nazis	32	14	12	107	230	196	288

The coalitions of von Papen and von Schleicher

Revised

In March 1932 Hitler stood against Hindenburg in the Presidential elections. He polled 13.4 million votes against 19.3 million cast for Hindenburg. Hitler was becoming a well-known figure in German politics and following the Nazi Party success in the July election he should have been appointed Chancellor. Hindenburg, however, despised him and instead appointed the Nationalist leader Franz von Papen as his Chancellor.

Unable to obtain a working majority, von Papen was forced to call another election in November when the Nazi vote fell and they obtained 196 seats, 34 less than July. As the Nazi Party was still the largest party in the Reichstag, Hitler again demanded the post of Chancellor and again he was denied it. This time Hindenburg turned to General von Schleicher, the Minister of Defence, and appointed him Chancellor. His attempts to form a working majority failed and in January 1933 von Papen managed to persuade Hindenburg to appoint a **Nazi-Nationalist government** with Hitler as Chancellor and von Papen as vice-Chancellor. Von Papen believed he could control Hitler as only three of the eleven cabinet seats would be held by Nazis.

On 30 January 1933 Adolf Hitler became Chancellor of Germany – he had attained power by legal and democratic means.

Key term

Nazi-Nationalist government – coalition of NSDAP (Nazi Party) and DNVP (German National People's Party) after January 1933

Revision task

Construct a timeline showing political developments in Germany between March 1930 and March 1933. Mark on unemployment figures, the presidential election, chancellors and governments.

German chancellors and their governments, 1930–33	
Brüning	March 1930–May 1932
Von Papen	May 1932–December 1932
Von Schleicher	December 1932–January 1933
Hitler–Von Papen	January 1933–March 1933

Reasons for the Nazi electoral success

Revised

By 1932 the Nazi Party was the largest party in the Reichstag and had attracted electoral support from all sections of German society. There were many reasons for this electoral success:

- **Impact of the Depression:** the onset of the Depression created the political and economic conditions that caused millions of Germans to switch their voting habits and vote for the extreme parties. The moderate parties which had formed the coalitions appeared unable to tackle the worsening economic conditions. What was needed was radical action and the Nazi Party seemed to offer this.

- **The appeal of Hitler:** Hitler was a gifted public speaker who captivated his audiences. He projected the image of being the messiah, the saviour who would solve the problems facing Germany. Using his private plane he toured the country delivering speeches to mass audiences, offering something to all sections of society. He kept his message simple, blaming scapegoats for Germany's problems, especially the Jews and communists.

- **Use of propaganda:** Dr Josef Goebbels was in charge of the party propaganda machine. Through staging mass rallies, huge poster campaigns, using the radio and cinema, he ensured that the Nazi message was hammered home.

- **Financial support:** the Nazi Party could not have financed its electoral campaigns without large-scale financial backing from big industrialists like Thyssen, Krupp and Bosch. These industrialists feared a communist takeover and were concerned at the growth of trade union power. Hitler promised to deal with both fears.

- **The use of the SA:** the SA played a vital role in protecting Nazi speakers during election meetings and also in disrupting the meetings of their political rivals, especially the Communists. These 'bully boy thugs' of the party engaged in street fights with the political opposition.

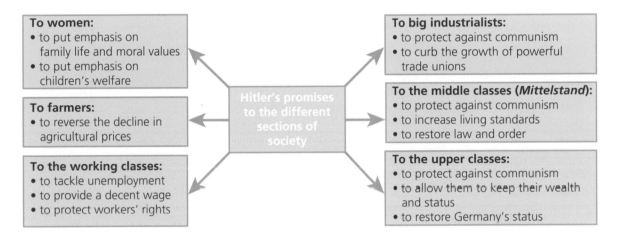

To women:
- to put emphasis on family life and moral values
- to put emphasis on children's welfare

To farmers:
- to reverse the decline in agricultural prices

To the working classes:
- to tackle unemployment
- to provide a decent wage
- to protect workers' rights

Hitler's promises to the different sections of society

To big industrialists:
- to protect against communism
- to curb the growth of powerful trade unions

To the middle classes (*Mittelstand*):
- to protect against communism
- to increase living standards
- to restore law and order

To the upper classes:
- to protect against communism
- to allow them to keep their wealth and status
- to restore Germany's status

Revision task

Copy and complete the following table explaining how each of the factors listed helped the Nazis to win votes in the general elections of the early 1930s.

	How it helped the Nazis win votes in the elections
Impact of the Depression	
Use of propaganda	
Financial support	
Use of the SA	
Appeal of Hitler	

Exam practice

How important was Hitler in attracting support for the Nazi Party in the elections of 1930 and 1932? **[6 marks]**

Answers online

Exam tip

In the 'how important' questions you need to identify two to three key reasons why something was important, using specific factual detail to back up your comments. In this instance you should refer to the appeal of Hitler as a public speaker, his promises to help particular groups in society and his leadership and direction of the Nazi Party. Remember to provide a judgement on 'how important'.

1.3 How did the Nazis consolidate their power, 1933–1934?

Between January 1933 and August 1934 Hitler turned Germany into a one-party **dictatorship**. By August 1934 the posts of Chancellor and President had been merged into a new post – Führer (leader). For the next twelve years Germany was ruled by a **totalitarian** regime known as the **Third Reich**.

The importance of the Reichstag Fire, 27 February 1933

Revised

When Hitler became Chancellor there were only two other Nazis in the Cabinet – Wilhelm Frick and Hermann Goering. Hitler's position was not strong as the Nazi-Nationalist alliance did not have a majority in the Reichstag. Hitler therefore persuaded Hindenburg to dissolve the Reichstag and call a general election for 5 March in which he hoped to increase the support for the Nazi Party. The Nazi propaganda machine helped deliver the party's message and the SA took to the streets to harass left-wing groups.

On 27 February, one week before the election, the Reichstag building was set on fire. A young Dutch Communist, Marinus van der Lubbe, was arrested and charged with starting the fire. Hitler used this event to his advantage:

- He argued that the Communists were planning a revolution.
- He persuaded Hindenburg to sign the 'Decree for the Protection of the People and State'.
- This gave Hitler the power to restrict free speech, limit the freedom of the press and imprison enemies of the state without trial.
- Communist and socialist newspapers were banned.

In the election on 5 March the Nazis won 288 seats but they still lacked an overall majority. A coalition was formed with the National Party. Hitler was disappointed as he needed two-thirds of the seats to be able to change the constitution, which was necessary to secure the passing of his Enabling bill.

The Enabling Act, 23 March 1933

Revised

On the day the Enabling bill was discussed in the Kroll Opera House (the temporary home of the Reichstag) Hitler banned the Communists from attending and encircled the building with SA men who prevented known opponents from entering. Absentees were counted as present and therefore in favour of the proposed bill. Promises were made by Hitler to the Catholic Centre Party to secure their votes. As a result the bill was passed, by 444 votes in favour to 94 against. Its passing marked the end of the Weimar Constitution. The Enabling Act became the 'foundation stone' of the Third Reich and it was used by Hitler to establish his dictatorship.

Use of the Enabling Act to establish the Nazi dictatorship

Revised

Through the use of the Enabling Act Hitler was able to establish his dictatorship and impose his policy of **gleichschaltung** (forcing into line):

Key term

Gleichschaltung – Nazi policy of forced coordination, bringing all social, economic and political activities under state control

Control of the states: on 30 January 1934 the Law for the Restoration of the Reich abolished state assemblies and replaced them with Reich governors.

Use of the Enabling Act

Purge of the civil service: on 7 April 1933 the Law for the Restoration of the Professional Civil Service removed Jews and political opponents of the Nazis from their posts in the civil service.

Control of the press: in October 1933 the Reich Press Law imposed strict control and censorship of the press.

Ban on political parties: on 14 July 1933 the Law against the Formation of Parties made the Nazi Party the only legal political party; Germany was now a one-party state; some parties had already disbanded voluntarily.

Trade Unions: on 2 May 1933 all trade unions were banned and replaced by the German Labour Front (Deutsche Arbeitsfront – DAF); strikes were made illegal.

The Night of the Long Knives, 30 June 1934

Revised

The SA had played a key part in the growth of the Nazi Party and as a reward their leader, Ernst Roehm, now wanted to incorporate the army into the SA. Roehm also wanted more government interference in the running of the country and he began pushing for a social revolution which would do away with Germany's class structure.

Hitler now saw the SA and its leadership as an increasing threat to his power. He needed the support of the army but the generals would never agree to Roehm's demands for the SA to control them. Hitler had to make a choice between the SA and the army. He decided on the latter and on the night of 30 June 1934 he used the SS to carry out a purge. Codenamed 'Operation Hummingbird', and known as the Night of the Long Knives, over 400 'enemies of the state' were arrested and shot by the SS. They included Roehm, former Chancellor von Schleicher and Bavarian Chief Minister von Kahr.

The importance of the Night of the Long Knives

Revised

The Night of the Long Knives is seen as a turning point in establishing Hitler's dictatorship:

- It eradicated would-be opponents to Hitler's rule.
- It secured the support of the army.
- It relegated the SA to a minor role.
- It provided Himmler with the opportunity to expand the SS.

The death of Hindenburg: Hitler becomes Führer

On 2 August 1934 President Hindenburg died. Hitler seized the opportunity to combine the two posts of President and Chancellor and gave himself the new title of Führer (leader). He was now Head of State and Commander-in-Chief of the Armed Forces. That same day the officers and men of the German army were made to swear an oath of loyalty to the Führer. In a referendum on 19 August more than 90 per cent of voters agreed with his action. Hitler was now absolute dictator of Germany.

Revision tasks

1. Copy and complete the following table to show how each factor helped to increase Hitler's power and control over Germany.

	How this factor helped to increase Hitler's power and control over Germany
Reichstag Fire	
Decree for Protection of the People and State	
Enabling Act	
Night of the Long Knives	
Death of Hindenburg	

2. Which of these events were the most important in making Hitler dictator of Germany? Rank them in order of their importance, giving reasons for your choice.

Exam practice

Source A: A cartoon by David Low which appeared in the British newspaper, the *London Evening Standard* on 3 July 1934. Goering is standing to Hitler's right, dressed as a Viking hero, and Goebbels is on his knees behind Hitler.

THEY SALUTE WITH BOTH HANDS NOW.

How far does Source A support the view that Hitler increased his power following the Night of the Long Knives? **[5 marks]**

Answers online

Exam tip

In the 'how far' questions you need to give a judgement on the accuracy of the information given in the source. In this instance you need to comment on how the SA leaders are lying dead having been shot and the remaining SA men have both their arms up in submission to Hitler. The German army is on Hitler's side. The source supports the viewpoint but it is a British cartoon and is therefore likely to be biased in its interpretation.

Chapter 2 Changing life for the German people, 1933–1939

Key issues

You will need to demonstrate good knowledge and understanding of the key issues of this period:

- How did Nazi economic and social policy affect life in Germany?
- How did Nazi political policy affect life in Germany?
- How did Nazi racial and religious policy affect life in Germany?

2.1 How did Nazi economic and social policy affect life in Germany?

Dealing with Germany's economic problems

Revised

When Hitler became Chancellor in January 1933 Germany had experienced more than three years of economic depression. Hitler immediately introduced a number of measures designed to reduce unemployment, which stood at 6 million.

- **Creation of the National Labour Service Corps (RAD):** from 1935 it was compulsory for all men aged 18–25 to serve in the RAD for six months, undertaking manual labour jobs. Workers lived in camps, wore uniforms and carried out military drill as well as work.

- **Public works programme:** men were put to work on public works schemes which included the building of 7000 km of autobahns (motorways), tree planting and the construction of hospitals, schools and houses.

- **Rearmament:** Hitler's decision to rearm transformed German industry and created jobs. Conscription was introduced in 1935 and the army was increased from 100,000 in 1933 to 1,400,000 in 1939. In 1933 3.5 billion marks was spent on producing tanks, aircraft and ships. By 1939 this figure had increased to 26 billion marks. Heavy industry expanded. Coal and chemical usage doubled between 1933 and 1939, while oil, iron and steel usage trebled.

- **Control of the economy:** in 1934 Hjalmar Schacht, President of the Reichsbank, was made Economic Minister. He believed in **deficit spending** to create jobs and used **Mefo bills** (credit notes) to finance public spending. In 1936 Schacht was replaced by Herman Goering as Economic Minister and he introduced the **Four-Year Plan** (1936–40). This was designed to speed up rearmament, prepare the country for war and establish the policy of **autarky** which was designed to make Germany self-sufficient, e.g. extracting oil from coal.

- **Invisible unemployment:** unemployment fell dramatically, from 6 million in 1933 to 350,000 by 1939 (see graph on page 22). However, these figures hid the true picture as they did not include Jews or women dismissed from their jobs, or opponents of the Nazi regime held in concentration camps.

Key terms

Deficit spending – when the government spends more money than it receives in order to expand the economy

Mefo bills – credit notes issued by the Reichsbank and guaranteed by the government. They were used to fund rearmament

Four-Year Plan – a plan which aimed to make Germany ready for war within four years, giving priority to rearmament and autarky

Autarky – a Nazi government policy of making Germany self-sufficient with no foreign imports

Revision task

Identify five factors which drove forward Germany's economic recovery after 1933. Rank them in order of importance.

- **Control of the workforce:** Hitler viewed trade unions as the breeding ground for socialism and communism. To avoid strikes and industrial unrest he banned the unions and in May 1933 replaced them with the German Labour Front (DAF). It had complete control over the discipline of workers, regulating pay and hours of work.
- **Rewarding the workforce:** to reward loyal workers the Strength through Joy (Kraft durch Freude – KdF) organisation was set up. It aimed to improve leisure time by sponsoring subsidised leisure activities and cultural events. These included concerts, theatre visits, sporting events, weekend trips, holidays and cruises. The Beauty of Work organisation aimed to improve working conditions through the building of canteens and sports facilities. In 1938 the Volkswagen (People's Car) Scheme was introduced, allowing workers to save five marks a week to buy their own car.

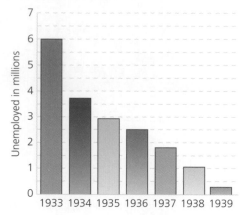

↑ **The fall in German unemployment, 1933–39**

Nazi attitudes and policies towards women

Revised

- **Progress made by women during the Weimar period:** during the Weimar period women made substantial advances in German society. They had achieved equal voting rights with men; they had been encouraged to obtain a good education and had taken up careers in the professions, especially in the civil service, law, medicine and teaching. German women (who chose to) could go out unescorted, follow fashion, wear make-up, smoke and drink in public.

- **Nazi attitudes towards women:** Nazi attitudes were very traditional and they introduced policies which reversed many of the gains made by women during the 1920s. The Nazis viewed men as the decision makers and political activists, while women were relegated to being responsible for the home and for bringing up children. They discouraged women from wearing make-up, trousers, high heels and from dyeing their hair.

> **Key term**
>
> **Aryan** – Nazi term for a non-Jewish German; someone of supposedly 'pure' German stock

- **Nazi policies aimed at women:**

The 'Three Ks'	Law for the Encouragement of Marriage (1933)	Lebensborn (Life Springs) Programme (1936)
Instead of going to work women were encouraged to stick to the 'Three Ks' (*Kinder, Küche, Kirche – Children, Kitchen, Church*). They were expected to give up their jobs, to get married and start a family.	This provided loans to encourage couples to marry, provided the wife left her job. Couples were allowed to keep one-quarter of the loan for each child born, up to four children. The Motherhood Cross medal was introduced to reward women with large families.	In an effort to boost the population, unmarried Aryan women were encouraged to 'denote a baby to the Führer' by becoming pregnant by 'racially pure' SS men.

Exam practice

Describe how life for women living in Germany changed between 1933 and 1939.　　　　**[4 marks]**

Answers online

Exam tip

In 'describe' questions you need to demonstrate specific knowledge, covering two to three key factors. In this instance you need to identify key areas of change in the lives of women, such as being forced to give up their jobs, adopting the lifestyle of the 'Three K's and being encouraged to have large families.

Nazi control of education

Revised

Hitler realised the importance of **indoctrinating** young people in Nazi beliefs. His aim was to turn them into loyal and enthusiastic supporters of the Third Reich. This was to be achieved through the control of education.

Key term

Indoctrinating – making someone accept a system of thought without question

- Teachers had to belong to the Nazi Teachers' League; they had to promote Nazi ideas in the classroom and swear an oath of loyalty to Hitler.
- The curriculum was strictly controlled: 15 per cent of the timetable was devoted to physical education; for the boys the emphasis was on preparation for the military; for the girls it was needlework and cookery to enable them to become good homemakers and mothers.
- Lessons started with pupils saluting and saying '*Heil* Hitler'. Every subject was taught through the Nazi point of view – biology lessons were used to study racial theory and the importance of the 'master race'; geography lessons were used to show how Germany was surrounded by hostile neighbours.
- Textbooks were rewritten to reflect Nazi views – history textbooks contained a heavy emphasis on German military glory and the evils of Communism and the Jews who were blamed for the problems of the Depression.

Nazi control of the German youth

Revised

The Nazis wanted to influence young people in school but also out of school. This was achieved through the Hitler Youth Movement which had existed since 1925. The Hitler Youth Law of 1936 made it difficult to avoid joining, blocking the promotion of parents who refused to allow their children to join. The Second Hitler Youth Law of 1939 made membership compulsory. By 1939 there were 7 million members. Baldur von Schirach was Reich Youth Leader.

There were several divisions of the Youth Movement, according to age:

Age	Boys	Girls
6–10	Pimpfen (Little Fellows)	
10–14	Jungvolk (Young Folk)	Jungmädel (Young Girls)
14–18	Hitler Jugend (Hitler Youth)	Bund Deutsche Mädchen (German Girls League)

- Boys were instructed in military skills such as shooting, map reading and drill; they took part in athletics, hiking and camping.
- Girls received physical training and learned domestic skills in preparation for motherhood and marriage; their groups had less emphasis on military training.

Revision task

How did the Nazis attempt to control young people:

- in school
- during their free time?

2.2 How did Nazi political policy affect life in Germany?

By the end of 1934 Hitler controlled the Reichstag, the army and the legal system. It was now almost impossible for anyone to escape the power and grip of the Nazis.

The Nazi Police State

By 1934 Germany was a police state and the key organs for ensuring conformity were:

- **The SS (Schutzstaffel):** formed in 1925 as a bodyguard for Hitler they were part of the SA. They wore black uniforms and after 1929 they were led by Heinrich Himmler. After the Night of the Long Knives (see page 19), the SS replaced the SA as the main security force, responsible for the removal of all opposition to the Nazis within Germany. SS officers had to be pure Aryans. By 1934 the SS numbered 50,000.
- **The Gestapo (Secret State Police):** set up by Goering in 1933, in 1936 they came under the control of the SS and were led by Himmler's deputy, Reinhard Heydrich. The Gestapo became feared as they could arrest and imprison suspected 'enemies of the state' without trial. Many of those arrested ended up in concentration camps. By 1939, 160,000 people were under arrest for political crimes.
- **Concentration camps:** the first concentration camp was opened in April 1933 at Dachau outside Munich and others soon followed at Buchenwald, Mauthausen and Sachsenhausen. Prisoners were classified into different categories and wore a coloured triangle to denote their crimes.

Control of the legal system

The Nazis aimed to control the courts and the legal system:

- Judges and lawyers had to belong to the National Socialist League for the Maintenance of Law and Order which forced them to accept Nazi policy. Those who refused were sacked.
- In October 1933 the German Lawyers Front was established and its 10,000 members swore an oath of loyalty to the Führer.
- In 1934 a new People's Court was set up to try enemies of the state. By 1939 it had sentenced over 500 people to death. The number of crimes punishable by death rose from 3 in 1933 to 46 in 1943. They included such crimes as listening to a foreign radio station.

Control of central and regional government

After 1933 Hitler reorganised central and regional government to ensure that all parts of it came under Nazi control:

- **Central government**: the Enabling Law (renewed every four years; see page 20) meant that the Reichstag was no longer needed to pass laws and it rarely met after 1933; Germany came to be governed by 'the will of the Führer' and Hitler made all the key decisions. Government policies were carried out by an elite core of Nazi leaders which included Hermann Goering, Josef Goebbels, Heinrich Himmler and, later, Martin Bormann. They competed to secure the attention of the Führer.

The Civil Service was purged of non-Nazis and carried out policies without question.

- **Regional government:** in March 1933 Hitler closed down all state parliaments and divided the country into regions (Gau), each headed by a Reich Governor (Gauleiter). These men were loyal party officials directly appointed by the Führer and they had the power to appoint and dismiss the town mayor and all councillors and make state laws.

Through these means Hitler maintained a tight hold over what went on at the central, regional and local levels of government.

The use of propaganda and censorship

In March 1934 the Ministry for Popular Enlightenment and Propaganda was set up under Dr Josef Goebbels. The aim of the organisation was to control the thoughts, beliefs and opinions of the German people. It attempted to brainwash them through a variety of methods:

- **Cinema:** all films had to be given pro-Nazi story lines and film plots had to be shown to Goebbels before going into production; shown with all films were official newsreels which glorified Hitler and Nazi achievements.

- **Newspapers:** all newspapers were subject to strict censorship and editors were told what they could print; the German people only read what the Nazis wanted them to know.

- **Rallies:** an annual mass rally of over 100,000 was staged in September at Nuremberg to showcase the Nazi regime; floodlights, stirring music, flags, banners and marching columns followed by a speech by Hitler created an atmosphere of frenzy; spectacular parades were held on other special occasions.

- **Radio:** all radio stations were placed under Nazi control; cheap mass-produced radios were sold; radio sets were placed in cafés and factories and loudspeakers broadcast programmes in the streets.

- **Posters:** great use was made of posters to put across the Nazi message.

- **Books:** all books were censored and those published had to put across the Nazi message; over 2500 writers were banned; in May 1933 Goebbels organised the burning of banned books through mass bonfires.

- **The arts:** music, painting, sculpture, the theatre and architecture all had to portray the Nazi interpretation of German life and society, emphasising the qualities of the 'master race' and its heroic citizens.

Exam practice

Explain why the use of propaganda and censorship was so important to the Nazi regime. **[5 marks]**

Answers online

Exam tip

In 'explain why' questions you need to give two or more reasons, supporting your answer with specific factual detail. In this instance you need to talk about the importance of controlling what the German people heard and read, and of using these methods to brainwash them into accepting Nazi views.

Revision task

Use the information in this section to explain how each of the following factors helped the Nazis gain control over the German people:

- Use of the SS and Gestapo
- Control of the legal system
- Control over central government
- Control over regional and local government

2.3 How did Nazi racial and religious policy affect life in Germany?

Nazi racial policy

The master race and the subhumans

In *Mein Kampf* Hitler had spelled out his ideas on race. He argued that pure Germans – Aryans – formed the 'master race' and they were characterised by being tall, having fair hair and blue eyes. However, over time this race had been contaminated by 'subhumans' – the *Untermenshen*. In order to rebuild the 'master race' as a pure line, it would be necessary to introduce selective breeding, preventing anyone who did not conform to the Aryan type from having children and, in extreme cases, eliminating them. Measures were introduced to sterilise the mentally ill, the physically disabled, homosexuals, black people and gypsies. Among those groups who received widespread persecution were the Jews.

The Nazi policy of anti-Semitism

Revised

Anti-Semitism goes back to the Middle Ages and attacks on Jews were common in Europe in the early twentieth century, particularly in Russia. The Nazis played on existing hatred and found a scapegoat in the Jews, blaming them for Germany's defeat in the First World War, the hyperinflation of 1923 and the economic depression of 1929. Hitler had no master plan to eliminate Germany of its Jews and until 1939 most of the measures introduced against the Jews were uncoordinated.

To begin with, Jews were encouraged to leave the country – in 1933 there were 550,000 Jews living in Germany, by 1939 280,000 had emigrated (including Albert Einstein who left for America in 1933). Life for German Jews got harsher as the 1930s progressed, starting with acts of public humiliation, until the Nazis eventually took away their human rights.

Measures taken against German Jews, 1933–39	
April 1933	Boycott of Jewish shops and businesses
April 1933	Jews banned from working in the Civil Service and holding positions such as teachers, doctors, dentists, judges
October 1933	Jews banned from working as journalists
May 1935	Jews banned from entering the armed forces
September 1935	The Nuremberg Laws: the Reich Law on Citizenship took away from Jews the right of German citizenship; the Law for the Protection of German Blood and Honour made it illegal for them to marry or to have sexual relations with Aryans
November 1936	Jews banned from using the German greeting 'Heil Hitler'
July 1938	Jews issued with identity cards; Jewish doctors, dentists and lawyers were forbidden to treat Aryans
August 1938	Jews forced to adopt the Jewish forenames of 'Israel' for a man and 'Sarah' for a woman
October 1938	Jewish passports had to be stamped with the large red letter 'J'
November 1938	Kristallnacht (Night of Broken Glass): the murder of a Nazi official in Paris by a young Polish Jew resulted in the events of 9–10 November. In reprisal for the murder, Goebbels organised attacks on Jewish property in cities across Germany; so many windows were smashed that the event became known as the 'Night of Broken Glass'; over 7500 Jewish shops were destroyed, 400 synagogues burnt down and about 100 Jews were killed; over 30,000 Jews were arrested and taken to concentration camps; Jews were fined 1 billion Reichmarks as compensation for the damage caused
December 1938	Forced sale of Jewish businesses
February 1939	Jews forced to hand over precious metals and jewellery
April 1939	Jews evicted from their homes and forced into ghettos

Revision task

Give five examples of how life for Jews living in Germany became more difficult after 1933.

Key term

Ghetto – part of a city inhabited by a minority because of social and economic pressure

Nazi attitudes towards religion

Hitler viewed the Church as a threat to Nazi policies but he also realised the importance of its support as Germany was a Christian country. Two-thirds of the population was Protestant and one-third was Catholic. Many Christians saw Nazism as a protection against the atheism of Communism and as an upholder of traditional family values and morals.

Nazi relations with the Catholic Church

In July 1933 Hitler signed a Concordat (agreement) with the Pope. This allowed the Catholic Church full religious freedom to operate without state interference and in return the Pope promised to keep the Church out of politics. Hitler soon broke this agreement – Catholic schools were taken out of Church control, Catholic youth groups were closed down and Catholic priests were harassed and arrested. In 1937 Pope Pius XI protested against the abuse of human rights. As a result 400 Catholic priests were arrested and sent to Dachau concentration camp.

Nazi relations with the Protestant Church

Many Protestants opposed Nazism and the **National Reich Church**. They were led by Pastor Martin Niemöller. In April 1934 he set up the Confessional Church which openly attacked the Nazi regime. In 1937 Niemöller was arrested and sent to a concentration camp. The Confessional Church was banned.

The creation of the National Reich Church

In 1933 the National Reich Church was set up to 'Nazify' the Protestant Church structure. It was led by Reich Bishop Ludwig Müller. The Bible, cross and other religious objects were removed from the altar and replaced with a copy of *Mein Kampf*, a portrait of the Führer and a sword. It seemed as if the Reich Church had been 'coordinated' through the process of *gleichschaltung* (see page 19). However, the Nazis never succeeded in destroying the Church in Germany. Priests and pastors had to make the choice of staying quiet and giving the appearance of conformity or being arrested by the Gestapo; most opted to support Hitler and conform.

> **Key term**
>
> **National Reich Church** – a new Nazi Church set up to attract worshippers away from traditional places of worship

> **Exam practice**
>
> The Nazis introduced changes which affected the lives of ordinary Germans. Did life under Nazi rule benefit all people living in Germany between 1933 and 1939?
>
> In your answer you should:
>
> - discuss those Germans who did benefit from Nazi rule
> - discuss those Germans who did not benefit from Nazi rule.
>
> **[10 marks + 3 marks for spelling, punctuation and grammar (SPaG)]**
>
> **Answers online**

> **Revision task**
>
> How far did the Nazis succeed in controlling the Church?

> **Exam tip**
>
> In the extended writing question you need to develop a two-sided answer which has balance and good factual support. In this instance you need to comment on those who benefited from the sharp fall in unemployment, the creation of jobs and reward schemes for loyal workers (KdF). You then need to comment on those who did not benefit, such as the Jews and gypsies for whom life grew more and more difficult. Remember to end with a clear judgement.

Chapter 3 War and its impact on life in Germany, 1939–1947

> **Key issues**
>
> You will need to demonstrate good knowledge and understanding of the key issues of this period:
>
> - How was life affected during the war years?
> - How much opposition was there to the Nazis within Germany during the war years?
> - What was the situation in Germany following total defeat in the war?

3.1 How was life affected during the war years?

A study of life on the **home front** can be divided into two phases. The first covered the years 1939–41 when the war was going well for Germany and there was only limited impact on the civilian population. The second phase covered the period 1942–45 when a number of key military defeats led to increasing economic hardship and social misery, culminating in the invasion of Germany by Allied forces and ultimate defeat.

> **Key terms**
>
> **Home front** – civilian life inside Germany during the war years
>
> **Blitzkrieg** – lightning war. The new method used by the German armed forces in 1939

Life during the early years of the war, 1939–41

Revised

- The success of the **blitzkrieg** tactics used by the German army in Poland and western Europe brought quick victories. These secured new supplies of raw materials as well as food and luxury goods which were sent back to Germany.
- Germany followed a policy of autarky by attempting to become self-sufficient. This meant the rationing of food, clothes and fuel which was introduced in 1939. The food ration cards had the unexpected result of imposing a healthier and more balanced diet on the German population.
- Fearing bombing raids, children were evacuated from Berlin in September 1940 but many soon returned. It was not until 1943 that mass evacuation of children took place, with Austria and Bavaria being the main destinations.
- All sections of society were encouraged to play a part in the war effort. The Hitler Youth became active in collecting metal, clothing and books for recycling.
- Although the Nazis believed a woman's place was in the home, more and more women were recruited into industry after 1937. They were needed to fill the places left by conscripted men. However, this did not become official policy until much later in the war.
- Goebbels made effective use of propaganda using the German victories of 1939–41 to boost morale at home and ensure support for the war effort.

Life during the later war years, 1942–45

Revised

- During 1942–43 Germany suffered several key defeats such as the battles of Stalingrad and El Alamein which meant the war was no longer going in her favour.

- In a speech in February 1943 Goebbels announced the policy of Total War, which meant ensuring all sections of the economy and society played a part in the war effort.

- To keep up morale Goebbels launched an intensive propaganda campaign. Posters played on the fear of Communism, offering the stark choice of 'Victory or Bolshevism'.

- In September 1943 Albert Speer was appointed Reich Minister for Armaments and Production. He quickly took direct control of the war economy, cutting the production of consumer goods and concentrating on war production. Productivity was increased and foreign workers were brought in to cover labour shortages. By 1944 29 per cent of all industrial workers were foreign.

- In 1943 the Nazis tried to mobilise women and 3 million women aged 17–45 were called to work. Only 1 million took up jobs.

- As defeats mounted, food shortages increased and in 1942 food rations were reduced. Parks and gardens in cities were dug up and used as vegetable patches. The short supply of goods led to illegal trading and a flourishing black market.

- In May 1943 Britain and the USA began a heavy bombing programme against German cities. The aim was to disrupt war production and destroy civilian morale. Berlin, Cologne, Hamburg and Dresden were all severely bombed. Millions of people were made homeless, many leaving the cities and becoming refugees. Raids on Dresden in February 1945 destroyed 70 per cent of all the buildings in the city and more than 150,000 civilians were killed in just two night attacks. Around 800,000 civilians were killed during the Allied bombing campaign.

- In September 1944 the Volkssturm, a people's home guard, was formed. It was to be used to defend Germany's cities against the Allied invasion. It was made up of men too old to serve in the army and boys from the Hitler Youth, who were all expected to provide their own uniforms and weapons. Its members lacked experience and were poorly trained. However, they did play an active role in the defence of central Berlin against the Russian invasion in April 1945.

Revision task

Copy and complete the following table to show the differences between the two phases of the war for life on the home front in Germany.

	1939–41	1942–45
Everyday life		
Food supplies/rationing		
Evacuation/city bombing		
Total War		
Morale/propaganda		
Volkssturm/Home Defence Force		

The Nazi treatment of Jews during the war years

Revised

Following the outbreak of war in 1939, the Nazi persecution of the Jews intensified but it did not follow any mapped-out plan. The policy evolved as the needs of war dictated.

- **Emigration:** the initial solution was forced emigration and at one point the French island of Madagascar was considered as an area for the resettlement of Europe's Jews.

- **Ghettos:** rapid German success in the early stages of the war caused the adoption of a more radical policy. The invasion of Poland brought 3 million Jews under Nazi control and Jews were herded into ghettos, the largest being in Warsaw. Surrounded by a large wall, conditions within the ghettos were extremely harsh. Overcrowding and meagre rations meant that thousands died of starvation, disease and the cold weather. Around 55,000 Jews died in the Warsaw ghetto.

- **Einsatzgruppen:** following the German invasion of the USSR in June 1941 another 5 million Jews came under Nazi control. Special killing squads known as Einsatzgruppen moved into the USSR behind the advancing German armies to round up and shoot Jews, burying them in mass graves. By 1943 such squads had murdered more than 2 million Jews.

- **Wannsee Conference:** on 20 January 1942 leading Nazis met at Wannsee in Berlin to work out a 'Final Solution' to the Jewish question. It was decided that death camps would be built in Poland and Jews from all over Nazi-occupied Europe would be transported there.

- **The Final Solution:** gas chambers and crematoria were built in camps at Auschwitz, Treblinka, Maidanek, Sobibor and Belzec in Poland. On arrival at these camps Jews were divided into two groups: those who were fit were forced to work to death in the labour camps; those labelled 'unfit' were sent directly to the gas chamber. Conditions within the camps were terrible. Those identified for work were fed very little food and they lived in cramped, filthy conditions where disease spread quickly. Their life expectancy was short. By the time the camps were liberated by the Allies in 1945 up to 6 million Jews and 500,000 gypsies had been worked to death, gassed or shot in what became known as the Holocaust.

Key terms

Einsatzgruppen – SS Special Action Squads responsible for the brutal killing of civilians in occupied territories

Final Solution – the Nazi plan for the systematic mass slaughter of Europe's Jews

Holocaust – mass slaughter, the Nazi murder of over 6 million Jews

Revision task

Make a copy of the following table. Use the information in this section to explain how and why Nazi policies towards the Jews grew harsher as the war progressed.

The treatment of the Jews during the war years, 1939–45		
Policy/action	Why this policy/action was adopted	What happened to the Jews as a result of this policy/action
Emigration		
Ghettos		
Einsatzgruppen		
Death camps and gas chambers		

Exam tip

In 'explain why' questions you need to give two or more reasons, supporting your answer with specific factual detail. In this instance you need to talk about how the Nazi invasions of Poland and the USSR brought millions of Jews under their direct control and consider the thinking behind the decisions made at the Wannsee Conference in January 1942.

Exam practice

Explain why the Nazis introduced the Final Solution programme in 1942. **[5 marks]**

Answers online

3.2 How much opposition was there to the Nazis within Germany during the war years?

As the war turned against Germany, resistance and opposition to the regime became more common, particularly from youth groups and religious leaders.

Opposition from young people

- **Edelweiss Pirates**: this group objected to the way the Nazis attempted to control the lives of young people. They wore check shirts and dark trousers and their emblem was the edelweiss flower. They beat up members of the Hitler Youth, pushed propaganda leaflets dropped by Allied planes through letterboxes, and sheltered deserters from the armed forces. Barthel Schink, the sixteen-year-old leader of the Cologne Pirates, together with twelve other members of this group, were hanged by the Gestapo in November 1944.

- **Swing Youth:** members tended to be middle class. They rejected the ideals of the Hitler Youth and developed a rival culture. Swing clubs were established in bars, nightclubs and houses in cities such as Hamburg, Berlin, Frankfurt and Dresden. They listened to British and American music, especially jazz.

Opposition from students

- **White Rose Group:** this was set up by Hans and Sophie Scholl and Professor Kurt Huber at Munich University in 1941. The group called for a campaign of passive resistance against the Nazi regime and distributed pamphlets to make people aware of Nazi atrocities. They painted anti-Nazi slogans on walls and on 18 February 1943 the leaders were arrested by the Gestapo for distributing anti-Nazi leaflets; they were tortured and hanged.

Exam practice

Source A: A pamphlet published by fifteen members of the White Rose Group at Munich University on 18 February 1943

'The day of reckoning has come. This is the day when German youth will get their revenge on Hitler. In the name of German youth we demand from Adolf Hitler the return of our personal freedom which he took from us. There can be but one word of action for us: Fight the Nazis. Each of us must join in the fight for our future. Students, the eyes of the German nation are upon us. The dead of Stalingrad beg us to act.'

How useful is Source A to a historian studying opposition to the Nazi regime during the Second World War? **[6 marks]**

Answers online

Exam tip

For the 'how useful' questions you need to make sure that your answers include reference to what the source actually says (its **Content**), that you identify who said this (its **Origin**) and that you refer to the circumstances under which it was written (its **Purpose**). This will enable you to make a judgement about whether the information is balanced or biased and if it is biased, why it is biased. Think: **COP**.

Opposition from religious groups

Once the true nature of the Nazi regime became apparent, opposition developed from individuals and groups within the Church.

- **Martin Niemöller** set up the Confessional Church in 1934 as an alternative to the National Reich Church. He frequently spoke out in public against the Nazi regime. He was eventually arrested and spent seven years in concentration camps.
- **Dietrich Bonhoeffer** was a Protestant pastor and member of the Confessional Church.

He spoke out critically against Nazi racist policies and helped Jews escape to Switzerland. He was arrested by the Gestapo in October 1942 and executed in April 1945.

- **Von Galen, the Catholic Archbishop of Munster**, spoke out critically against the Nazi euthanasia policy, Gestapo terror and concentration camps. He became known as the 'Lion of Munster' but was arrested following the July Bomb Plot of 1944 (see below).

Opposition to Nazi rule from the military   Revised

- **General Ludwig Beck and his circle**: Beck resigned from his post in the army because he disagreed with Hitler's plans to challenge the Versailles settlement. Together with Karl Goerdeler, a Nazi official, they gathered together a circle which organised two failed assassination attempts on Hitler's life in March and November

1943. They also played a leading role in the July Bomb Plot.

- **Colonel Claus von Stauffenberg and the July Bomb Plot, 1944**: this was the closest the German military came in attempting to assassinate Hitler.

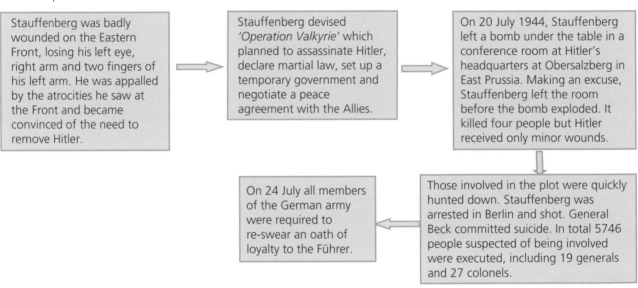

Stauffenberg was badly wounded on the Eastern Front, losing his left eye, right arm and two fingers of his left arm. He was appalled by the atrocities he saw at the Front and became convinced of the need to remove Hitler.

Stauffenberg devised 'Operation Valkyrie' which planned to assassinate Hitler, declare martial law, set up a temporary government and negotiate a peace agreement with the Allies.

On 20 July 1944, Stauffenberg left a bomb under the table in a conference room at Hitler's headquarters at Obersalzberg in East Prussia. Making an excuse, Stauffenberg left the room before the bomb exploded. It killed four people but Hitler received only minor wounds.

On 24 July all members of the German army were required to re-swear an oath of loyalty to the Führer.

Those involved in the plot were quickly hunted down. Stauffenberg was arrested in Berlin and shot. General Beck committed suicide. In total 5746 people suspected of being involved were executed, including 19 generals and 27 colonels.

↑ **The July Bomb Plot, 1944**

Revision task

Make a copy of the following table. Use the information in this section to describe the type of opposition to Nazi rule that emerged within Germany during the war years and how it was dealt with.

Opposition to Nazi rule during the war years, 1939–45			
	Name of group/ individual	**Examples of opposition displayed by this group/ individual**	**How such opposition was dealt with by the Nazi authorities**
Young Germans			
University students			
Religious leaders			
German military			

3.3 What was the situation in Germany following total defeat in the war?

By early 1945 it was clear that Germany had lost the war. The Allies were advancing through Germany on both the Eastern and the Western Fronts and, by April, Berlin was under attack.

Developments on the Eastern Front, 1943–45 Revised

- 1942–43 was the turning point in the war on the Eastern Front, when the Germans failed to take the city of Stalingrad and surrendered their forces.
- In July 1943 the Germans were defeated at the Battle of Kursk, losing 2000 tanks. The Soviet Union now began to advance westwards at a rapid rate.

- By the end of 1944 all German troops had been pushed out of the Soviet Union.
- Soviet forces liberated Warsaw in Poland on 17 January 1945, Budapest in Hungary on 11 February and Vienna in Austria on 13 April.
- By mid April 1945 Soviet forces were threatening Berlin.

Developments on the Western Front, 1943–45 — Revised

- By 1943 the Germans were losing the Battle of the Atlantic and their U-boats were no longer a major threat.
- On 6 June 1944, D-Day, Allied forces landed on the Normandy beaches, opening up a second front (the Western Front) in the attack on German forces.
- After capturing the beachheads Allied forces advanced through France, liberated Paris on 25 August and pushed on into Belgium.
- In December 1944 German forces launched a counter-attack through the Ardennes (the Battle

of the Bulge) and to begin with they broke through the American lines. However, they were eventually pushed back.
- Heavy bombing raids by the RAF and USAAF during 1943–45 destroyed industrial sites, roads, bridges and rail networks across Germany, causing disruption to the German war effort.
- On 9 March 1945 Allied forces crossed the River Rhine at Remagen and entered Germany, hoping to get to Berlin before the Soviets did.

The fall of Berlin, April 1945 — Revised

- On 16 April the Soviet attack on Berlin started. It involved 1.5 million men, 6300 tanks and 8500 aircraft.
- By 24 April Berlin was surrounded and fierce house-to-house fighting took place. About 100,000 members of the Volkssturm attempted to defend the city.

- On 2 May General Weidling, the defence commandant of Berlin, ordered the surrender of German forces defending the city.
- Over 300,000 Soviet troops had been killed or wounded in the battle for Berlin.

The death of Hitler and the German surrender — Revised

- Hitler spent his last days in an underground bunker in the Reich Chancellery.
- At midnight on 28 April he married Eva Braun.
- In his political testament he left the leadership of Germany split between Admiral Dönitz and Goebbels.
- On 30 April Hitler and Braun committed suicide; afterwards their bodies were wrapped in a

blanket, taken outside the bunker, soaked in petrol and burnt.
- On 1 May Goebbels committed suicide.
- On 4 May Hitler's remains were found by Soviet troops and taken away for examination.
- On 8 May Dönitz agreed to the Allied terms of unconditional surrender which ended the war and the Third Reich.

The condition of Germany at the end of the war

Revised

- Around 3.25 million soldiers and 3.6 million civilians had been killed.
- The country was swarming with refugees.
- More than 25 per cent of all homes had been destroyed.
- Almost all major towns and cities lay in ruins.
- The economy was in ruins – money was worthless and had been replaced by bartering.

Revision tasks

1. Explain the importance of each of the following events in the downfall of the Third Reich.

   - Battle of Stalingrad
   - Battle of Kursk
   - D-Day
   - Battle of Berlin
   - Death of Hitler
   - Unconditional surrender

2. Write a paragraph to describe the condition of Germany in May 1945.

The punishment of a defeated Germany

A key aim of the Allies was to prevent Germany from ever being able to threaten the peace of Europe again. Decisions about the future of Germany were made at two important conferences.

The Yalta Conference, February 1945

Revised

In February 1945 the three Allied leaders, Churchill, Roosevelt and Stalin, met at Yalta in the Crimea to consider what to do with Germany once the Nazi regime was defeated. It was decided that Germany was to be divided into four zones of occupation (British, French, American and Soviet zones). Berlin was also to be divided into these four zones. It was agreed to hunt down Nazi war criminals and to allow countries liberated from Nazi rule to have free elections to decide their future government.

The Potsdam Conference, July 1945

Revised

A second conference was held at Potsdam on the outskirts of Berlin in July. Tensions between the Allies were emerging as the Soviets showed no signs of withdrawing from Eastern Europe. The division of Germany and Berlin agreed at Yalta was confirmed and it was also agreed to demilitarise the country, ban the Nazi Party, begin the process of denazification and put Nazi leaders on trial.

Key term

Denazification – attempt to remove Nazi influence

The Nuremberg Trials

Revised

On 21 November 1945, 22 senior ranking Nazis and 200 other Nazis were put on trial at Nuremberg. They were charged with waging war, committing crimes against peace and humanity, and war crimes. The trials lasted until 1 October 1946, with 142 people being found guilty and 24 receiving death sentences (eleven of which were later amended to life imprisonment). Goering cheated the hangman by committing suicide the night before his execution.

Policy of denazification

Revised

This was a deliberate policy of removing traces of the Nazi regime from German society, culture, press, economy, judiciary and politics. It was achieved through a series of directives issued by the Allied Control Council and included the following actions:

- **10 October 1945** – the National Socialist Party was dissolved and its revival totally prohibited.
- **1 December 1945** – all German military units dissolved.
- **12 January 1946** – issue of criteria for the removal from public office of anybody who had played more than a nominal role in Nazi Party activities. Special courts were set up to determine the extent of involvement of Party members in the Nazi regime. However, it proved impossible to examine all Party members thoroughly and many escaped justice.
- **13 May 1946** – confiscation of all media associated with Nazism or militarism. Over 30,000 books were banned.

Germany in 1947

Revised

By 1947 the division between East and West Germany was beginning to appear. In the western zones (British, French, American) capitalism and democracy were being introduced, and in the eastern zone (Soviet) communism was emerging as the dominant force. Churchill used the phrase 'Iron Curtain' to describe the division emerging between East and West. In 1949 two separate countries were created from the occupation zones – the three western zones merged to form the Federal Republic of Germany, while the eastern zone formed the German Democratic Republic. The two countries of East and West Germany continued to exist until reunification in 1990.

Revision task

Copy and complete the chart below to show how the Allies dealt with Germany after the defeat of the Third Reich.

How the Allies dealt with Germany after the defeat of the Third Reich	
Decisions made at Yalta and Potsdam	
Nuremberg Trials	
Policy of denazification	
Situation in Germany in 1947	

Exam practice

Source A: The division of Germany and Berlin in 1948

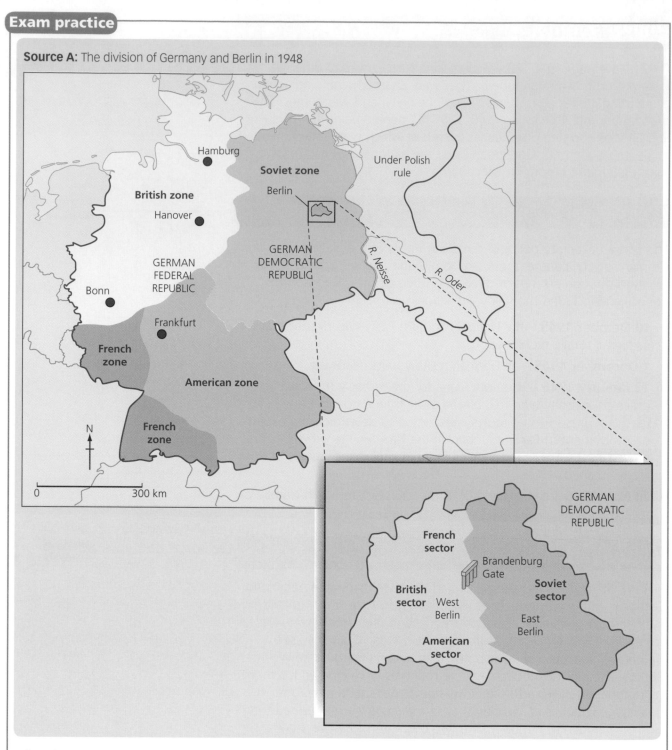

What does Source A show you about Germany after 1945?

[2 marks]

Answers online

Exam tip

In this type of question you need to pick out specific detail from what you can see in the source and from the caption attached to it. In this context you need to say that the map shows that Germany was divided into zones, each controlled by an Allied power. Berlin was also divided. It is important that you *'say what you see'*.

Chapter 4 The growth and development of sport in Wales and England

> **Key issues**
>
> You will need to demonstrate good knowledge and understanding of the key issues of this period:
>
> - What were the main characteristics of sport up to 1945?
> - How important was the contribution of sporting heroes during this period?
> - How has sport in Wales and England been affected by changes in society since 1950?

4.1 What were the main characteristics of sport up to 1945?

The distinction between amateur and professional sport

Revised ☐

During the early part of the twentieth century there was a distinction between amateur and professional sport, often linked to **social class**.

- **Amateur** sport was played as a pastime and not for money. It was best seen in rowing (Henley Regatta), tennis (Wimbledon) and horse racing (Royal Ascot). These sports tended to be dominated by the middle and upper classes.
- **Professional** sport was played to earn money. This began to appear in sports such as football, cricket and boxing. These sports were popular with the working classes who needed money to make up for time not in work.

> **Key terms**
>
> **Social class** – the division in society based on a person's background and income
>
> **Amateur (in sport)** – someone who participates or follows a sport for the love of it and not for money
>
> **Professional (in sport)** – someone who earns a living by being paid to play a particular sport

The battle between amateurism and professionalism: rugby

Revised ☐

- **Rugby Union** had spread from English public schools and universities in the mid-nineteenth century.
- In 1895 the 'broken-time' issue split the game. Rugby Union organisers refused demands for players to be paid for time off work; this led to the creation of the **Rugby League**, which allowed professional playing.
- Rugby League became very popular in the industrial towns of northern England and the Midlands. Wales, however, favoured Rugby Union.

> **Key terms**
>
> **Rugby Union** – rugby played by amateurs; the players were not paid
>
> **Rugby League** – rugby that was always professional; the players were paid

- Rugby Union suffered badly in Wales during the 1930s Depression when many talented players joined professional clubs in northern England.
- Rugby Union did not allow professional playing until the late twentieth century.

The battle between amateurism and professionalism: football

Revised

- Association football (what we now call football rather than soccer) was very popular across England and Wales by 1900.
- It was a game largely played and supported by working-class people.
- The Football Association (established 1863) allowed players to be paid a wage in 1863, and in 1901 set a weekly maximum of £4.
- By 1900, in Wales, football was most popular in the north-east, the closest area to the industrial towns of the north and midlands of England; one of the earliest teams in Wales was Wrexham Football Club, founded in 1872.
- By the 1920s football had become popular across the South Wales valleys and in 1927 Cardiff City won the FA Cup Final.
- After experiencing a downturn during the Depression, the game had revived by the end of the 1930s, with increasing radio and press coverage helping to boost its appeal.
- Professional players began to emerge as 'sports stars'.
- The **football pools** started in the early 1920s.

The battle between amateurism and professionalism: boxing

Revised

- Boxing has a long history; travelling fairs often had **fighting booths**.
- It became a popular betting sport among both rich and poor.
- Boxing was generally poorly paid, with most boxers earning between £2 and £4 per fight.
- In August 1937 the boxer Tommy Farr, from Rhondda in Wales, was unsuccessful in his attempt to take the world heavyweight title from the American boxer Joe Louis, but he earned £10,000 for the fight.

Key terms

Football pools – a means of betting on the results of football matches

Fighting booth – a fairground attraction that allowed ordinary men to box a 'pro' and earn a few shillings if they won

The battle between amateurism and professionalism: cricket

Revised

- Cricket was regarded as the national sport of England. There was a sharp distinction between the amateur 'gentlemen' and professional 'players'; they had separate dressing rooms and hotels, and travelled in separate railway carriages.
- By the turn of the twentieth century most English towns had their own local amateur cricket teams.
- Cricket created some of Britain's first sporting heroes; professional players such as Jack Hobbs and Wally Hammond dominated the sport in the interwar years.
- Huge crowds watched international **test matches**, especially the fight for **the Ashes** trophy between England and Australia.

Key terms

Test match – an international match, usually one of a series

The Ashes – test matches in cricket held between England and Australia

The battle between amateurism and professionalism: golf and tennis

Revised

- At the start of the twentieth century golf was dominated by the wealthy. Private golf clubs with restricted membership rules emerged.
- In spite of this, golf was more advanced than other sports as it allowed amateurs and professionals to play alongside each other, and, by the 1920s, women played too.
- Lawn tennis was for richer people who had private courts; the spread of middle-class suburbs led to the creation of clubs like Garden Village in Wrexham and Dinas Powys in Cardiff.
- After the First World War, many councils began to build grass and hard tennis courts in public parks.
- The success of Fred Perry, who won the singles title at Wimbledon three times in a row (1934–36), was a great boost to tennis.

The battle between amateurism and professionalism: other sports

Revised

- Greyhound racing became popular in the 1930s. Popular venues included the White City track in London and Belle Vue in Manchester. In 1933 over 6 million spectators visited greyhound racing tracks.
- Cycling became popular during the interwar years; cycling clubs sprang up across the country. In 1935 over 4 million bicycles were sold.
- Speedway (motorcycle) racing began in the late 1920s and attracted large crowds during the 1930s.
- Sport tended to be dominated by men and there were few opportunities for women. Upper- and middle-class women took part in genteel sports like tennis, golf and croquet; working-class women lacked the time or the money to participate.

Revision tasks

Use the information in this section to complete the following.

1. Explain the difference between amateurism and professionalism in sport.

2. Give examples of how the growth of professionalism affected each of the following sports:

Rugby	Association football	Cricket
Boxing	Golf	Tennis

Exam practice

Source A: The entry for Rugby League that was printed in the *Encyclopaedia for Wales* (2008). The entries in the encyclopaedia are written by professional historians.

'Begun in 1895, when leading north of England clubs withdrew from the Rugby Football Union after being refused the right to compensate players for the loss of earnings, Rugby League rapidly evolved into a separate game, permitting open professionalism and, in 1907, reducing teams from 15 players to 13. The League's existence provided an opportunity for players to cash in on their skills.'

How useful is Source A to a historian studying the growth of professionalism in the game of rugby? **[6 marks]**

Answers online

Exam tip

For the 'how useful' questions you need to ensure that your answers include reference to what the source actually says (its **Content**), that you identify who said this (its **Origin**) and that you refer to the circumstances under which it was written (its **Purpose**). This will enable you to judge whether the information is balanced or biased, and if it is biased, why. Think: **COP**.

The growth of spectator sport

Revised

The first half of the twentieth century saw a massive increase in the numbers of spectators. Several factors explain this dramatic growth:

Increased leisure time
The **Bank Holiday** Act 1871 meant sports matches could be arranged on Good Friday, Easter Monday, Christmas Day and Boxing Day when large crowds could attend; most workers had Saturdays or Saturday afternoons off which enabled them to watch.

Influence of the radio
The British Broadcasting Corporation (BBC) (see page 51) began live outdoor broadcasts of sporting fixtures in the 1920s; events like the University Boat Race, the Derby, boxing matches and cricket tests attracted large radio audiences.

Rivalries between regions
Derby matches in football and rugby attracted large crowds; the 'Roses' cricket fixtures between Lancashire and Yorkshire were popular events, as were the rugby internationals between the home nations.

Reasons for the growth of spectator sport in the early twentieth century

Better transport
The spread of the railway network meant spectators could travel easily and cheaply to support their teams; railway companies ran 'special' trains just for spectators; the growth of motorised transport in the 1930s made commuting easier.

Competitions and tournaments
Tournaments such as Wimbledon and the Ashes became very popular; the Football League grew (Division 2 was added in 1898 and Divisions 3 north and south in 1921); Rugby Union had its Home International and Five Nations (set up in 1910) tournaments; Rugby League began its own league in 1922.

Attraction of sporting heroes
The 1920s and 1930s saw the appearance of 'sporting heroes' who drew large crowds; these included the tennis player Fred Perry, the cricketers Jack Hobbs and Wally Hammond, the boxer Tommy Farr and the racing greyhound 'Mick the Miller'.

Revision task

For each of the following factors use the information in this section to give two reasons explaining how they contributed to the growth in spectator sport:

Leisure time   Radio   Transport   Sporting heroes

Key terms

Bank holiday – a guaranteed public holiday

Derby match – a game played between teams from neighbouring places

4.2 How important was the contribution of sporting heroes during this period?

The influence of the media up to the 1970s

Revised

The media hugely influenced the development of sport up to the 1970s:

- They encouraged a following of certain sports.
- They helped create the image of sporting heroes.

It was a two-way process: sport needed media coverage to generate interest and a loyal following, and the media needed sport to attract readers and listeners.

A range of media types – both written and unwritten – have been used to report on sporting events and personalities.

Newspapers

- Some newspapers were completely dedicated to sport, for example *Sporting Life,* a daily paper which covered all sporting events.
- After the Second World War, dailies and Sunday papers expanded their news reporting, some bringing out late editions to cover the day's sporting results.
- Newspapers devote specific pages to sport and tend to concentrate on high-profile sports like football, cricket, horse racing, boxing and rugby.
- Journalists specialise in sports commentary – Neville Cardus reported on cricket for the *Manchester Guardian* during the first half of the twentieth century; former cricketer Sir Leonard Hutton wrote columns for the *London Evening News* in the 1950s.
- Specialist sports photographers, such as Tony Duffy, developed during the 1950s and 1960s.

Magazines

Several magazines devoted to sport issues began to circulate:

- *The Cricketer* magazine was first published in 1921.
- *The Topical Times* was a weekly magazine, which appeared between 1919 and 1940 and contained articles on football, boxing and horse racing.
- *The Football Pictorial and Illustrated Review* first appeared in 1935.
- The *Sport Weekly Magazine* began publication in 1938.
- England's World Cup victory in 1966 led to a surge of football magazines; one of the most successful, *Shoot,* began in 1969.

Comics

Comics featured fictional sports stars who had tremendous appeal, especially with boys:

- The athletic runner Alf Tupper first appeared in the *Rover* in 1949 and continued to appear for the next 40 years.
- The character Roy of the Rovers launched his football career in 1954 in the *Tiger*; in 1976 he went on to have his own weekly comic.
- The character Billy from the comic strip *Billy's Boots* began his football career in the *Scorcher* in 1970 and in 1974 moved to the *Tiger.*

Radio

The radio played an important role in developing the popularity of sport from the 1930s onwards. In 1948 the BBC began broadcasting *Sports Report* at 5.00p.m. on a Saturday, providing football results and brief reports of top matches. Other sporting events like horse racing, Wimbledon and the Boat Race attracted large audiences.

Television

Television coverage of sport really developed in the 1960s when the BBC and ITV began broadcasting Saturday afternoon sports programmes. The 1966 World Cup Final when England beat West Germany 4–2 attracted 32.6 million viewers.

- The BBC programme *Grandstand* ran from 1958 to 2007 and covered all sporting events; commentators like David Coleman, Eddie Waring and Murray Walker became **household names**; in 1964 the BBC launched the successful *Match of the Day* programme.
- In the mid-1960s ITV launched its *World of Sport* and added to this in 1968 with *The Big Match.*

> **Key term**
>
> **Household names** – sports or media stars who became well known

Cinema

From the 1920s to the 1960s (when TV took over), the cinema showed **newsreels** between films, which covered sporting events and details about the lives of sports personalities. Such coverage helped create sporting icons and celebrities.

Revision task

Copy out the table below and use the information in this section to complete it.

Media type	How this media type helped the development of sport
Newspapers	
Magazines	
Comics	
Radio	
Television	

Exam practice

Source A: From a specialist history book on sport published in 2007

'Between the wars soccer [football] was the leading national sport in Britain. But far more people watched the brief clips of soccer on the newsreels in the cinema than ever watched football on the pitch. Newsreels were a crucial factor in the development of football as a mass sport, making stars of hundreds of players.'

Use the information in Source A and your own knowledge to explain why cinema newsreels were important in the growth in popularity of sport up to the 1970s. **[4 marks]**

Answers online

Exam tip

This type of question requires you to do two things: discuss the content of the source and add additional points from your own knowledge. In this instance the source talks about how more people went to the cinema than attended football matches. You could add that through regular attendance they became familiar with specific sports and sports stars.

Sporting stars and their impact

Through coverage in the media – newspapers, radio, cinema and TV – sports stars developed huge followings of loyal fans. Some became major stars, developing cult status within their respective sports. Some have gone on to become great ambassadors for their sport, encouraging others to participate or become spectators.

Key term

Paralympic Games – an international tournament for physically disabled athletes

Revision task

Look at the tables on the opposite page. For each of the following sports personalities, use the information in this section to explain why they became 'major stars' within their particular sport: Fred Perry; Mary Rand; Len Hutton; Tanni Grey-Thompson; Gareth Edwards; Kelly Holmes; David Beckham; Nicole Cooke.

Revised

Tennis	Fred Perry (1909–95)	● Greatest UK tennis player of the twentieth century
		● Won Wimbledon three years in a row (1934–36)
		● Was World No 1 in tennis for four years
		● First player to win all four Grand Slam singles titles
		● Great ambassador for the game of tennis
Cricket	Len Hutton (1916–90)	● Wisden's *Cricketers' Almanack* described him as one of the greatest batsmen in the history of cricket
		● Set the record in 1938 for the highest individual innings in a Test match, scoring 364 runs against Australia
		● England's first professional captain, holding the captaincy from 1952 to 1955
		● Knighted for his contribution to cricket in 1956
Rugby	Gareth Edwards (1947–)	● Played scrum-half for Wales during the 1960s and 1970s
		● His try against the Barbarians in 1973 has been hailed as the greatest try ever
		● Described by the BBC as 'the greatest player ever to don a Welsh jersey'
		● Awarded the CBE in 2007 for his services to sport
Football	David Beckham (1975–)	● One of Britain's most successful midfielders
		● Captain of England's football team for six years
		● First British footballer to play 100 Champions League matches
		● Was runner-up twice for FIFA World Player of the Year
		● Awarded the OBE in 2003 for his services to sport
		● A global celebrity and a national icon

Revised

Athletics	Mary Rand (1940–)	● The first British woman to win a gold medal in athletics (1964 Tokyo Olympics)
		● The only woman to win three medals in a single Olympic Games – gold for long jump, silver for pentathlon and bronze for 100m relay
		● Voted BBC Sports Personality of the Year for 1964
		● Held the world record for the triple jump from 1959 to 1981
		● Became the first 'Golden Girl' of British athletics
Para-lympics	Tanni Grey-Thompson (1969–)	● Considered to be one of the most successful disabled athletes in the UK
		● Won 16 medals (including 11 golds) at the **Paralympic Games**
		● Held 30 world records and won the London Marathon six times between 1992 and 2002
		● Awarded the MBE and OBE for services to sport, and made a Dame in 2005
		● An active ambassador for disability sport
Athletics	Kelly Holmes (1970–)	● A middle-distance runner, she won two gold medals in the Athens Olympics in 2004, becoming the first woman to win two golds in a single Games
		● Won silver and bronze medals in the World Championships and European Championships, and a gold and silver in the Commonwealth Games
		● Won the BBC Sports Personality of the Year in 2004, and made a Dame in 2005
Cycling	Nicole Cooke (1983–)	● Wales' greatest female cyclist
		● Won gold in the 2008 Beijing Olympics
		● Won medals in the Commonwealth and World road race championships
		● The first cyclist to become road race world champion and Olympic gold medallist in the same year
		● Voted BBC Wales Sports Personality of the Year in 2003
		● Awarded the MBE in 2009

4.3 How has sport in Wales and England been affected by changes in society since 1950?

There were increased opportunities for participation in sport and recreational activities in the late twentieth century, caused by a number of factors.

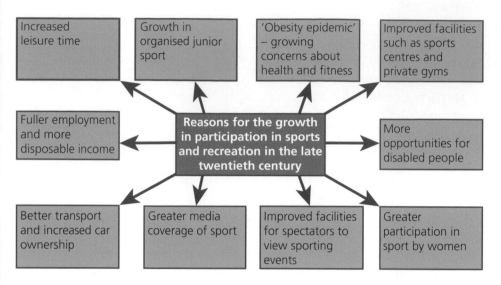

Increased leisure time

Growth in organised junior sport

'Obesity epidemic' – growing concerns about health and fitness

Improved facilities such as sports centres and private gyms

Fuller employment and more disposable income

Reasons for the growth in participation in sports and recreation in the late twentieth century

More opportunities for disabled people

Better transport and increased car ownership

Greater media coverage of sport

Improved facilities for spectators to view sporting events

Greater participation in sport by women

Increased leisure time

Revised

Since the end of the Second World War, the standard of living for ordinary people has improved. Holiday time and disposable income have increased. Wider car ownership has made the population more mobile and made it easier for people to participate in sports. Although women generally tend to have less free time than men, the success of female athletes at Olympic Games has encouraged more women to participate in sport.

Improved facilities

Revised

The late twentieth century saw a growth in sports centres, which encouraged people to participate in a range of sports not previously available.

- The first purpose-built sports centre in England opened at Harlow in Essex in 1964.
- The Wales Institute of Sport opened in Cardiff in 1971.
- Sports such as basketball, volleyball, badminton and squash grew in popularity.
- The introduction of floodlights allowed training and games in the evenings throughout the year.

- The development of synthetic outdoor playing surfaces in the 1970s and 1980s improved opportunities for participation – sports like hockey, tennis and football benefited from this.
- Events such as the death of 95 Liverpool football fans in the Hillsborough Stadium disaster in 1989 resulted in improved facilities; many football clubs like Sunderland, Swansea and Cardiff moved to new all-seater stadiums; the National Stadium in Cardiff was demolished in 1997 to build the Millennium Stadium to host the 1999 Rugby World Cup.

The impact of the 'obesity epidemic'

During the late twentieth century, medical and government officials became concerned about a possible **obesity epidemic**. They believed that several factors were making this more likely – people adopting a less active lifestyle, the impact of supermarket shopping, and an increased reliance on **'junk foods'** (especially among the young). Attempts to combat the obesity problem have included the development of sporting complexes:

- New sports centres have been built which provide a range of activities such as fitness suites and gyms, swimming pools, badminton and squash courts, and football pitches.
- **Private gyms** have opened up across the country and become very popular.
- Activity centres have opened, such as Plas Menai in North Wales (opened in 1986); it offers facilities such as white water rafting, canoeing, sailing, caving, rock climbing and mountain biking.

Key terms

'Obesity epidemic' – a trend towards many people becoming heavily overweight

Junk food – ready prepared food that is low in nutritional value

Private gyms – sporting facilities where people pay a membership fee to use them

Disability sports

- Sport was introduced as a form of rehabilitation for injured ex-service people after the Second World War.
- The 1948 Olympic Games in London resulted in the introduction of sports competitions for wheelchair athletes at the Stoke Mandeville hospital.
- The Stoke Mandeville Games evolved into the modern Paralympic Games – athletes like Tanni Grey-Thompson and Eleanor (Ellie) Simmons became well-known through their involvement in the Games.
- Local authorities have worked with specialist organisations to improve sporting facilities for disabled people but progress has been slow.

The growth in organised junior sports

Although schools have continued to teach physical education, in recent decades the number of matches played between schools has declined. To fill this gap, local sports clubs like football, hockey, cricket and rugby clubs have started to coach and organise junior teams of all ages and both sexes. National youth movements such as the Young Farmers' Clubs and the **Urdd Gobaith Cymru** have introduced sports competitions into their festivals.

Key term

Urdd Gobaith Cymru – a youth movement for young people in Wales

Revision task

Copy out the table below and use your knowledge to complete each section.

Factor	How developments in this area contributed to the growth in the number of people participating in sport
Improved facilities	
Obesity epidemic	
Disability sport	
Junior sport	

Exam practice

What does Source A show you about sports facilities on offer in Wales between 1972 and 1997? **[2 marks]**

Source A: Figures showing increasing sports facilities in Wales, 1972–97

Facility	1972	1997
Sports halls	11	180
Swimming pools	25	143
Squash courts	86	442
Indoor tennis centres	0	9
Artificial pitches	0	72
Indoor bowls halls	0	27
Ice rinks	0	2

Exam tip

In this type of question you need to look into the source and pick out relevant details, including the caption. Aim to write two sentences. In this instance the source shows dramatic increases in sports facilities between 1972 and 1997. This made it easier for people to participate in sport.

Key term

Twenty20 – where two cricket teams each have a single innings, batting for a maximum of twenty overs

The influence of television and sponsorship in the late twentieth century

The impact of live TV coverage

Revised

Live television coverage had a tremendous impact on the development of sport during the late twentieth century.

- By the 1960s the majority of households had access to a television.
- Sports events broadcasts helped to develop a growing interest in sport and also encouraged people to take up that sport as a hobby.
- TV has helped to turn one-time minority sports into nationwide favourites:
  - The BBC programme *Pot Black* helped make snooker a popular sport on TV during the 1970s and 1980s, making household names of players such as Steve Davies, Dennis Taylor and Alex 'Hurricane' Higgins.
  - TV coverage of darts championships made household names of players like Eric Bristow and Jocky Wilson.
- Events like the London Marathon, Formula One, Wimbledon, the Open, the Grand National and the Boat Race have become essential parts of

the sporting calendar, with TV coverage allowing audiences to view these events live.
- Satellite and cable TV have raised the profile of once little-known sports like American football, basketball and beach volleyball.
- Larger audiences have helped attract major sponsors who have used sport as a form of advertising, pumping money into the sponsored sport as a result.
- Sponsorship, together with satellite TV, has changed many 'traditional' sports – cricket, for example, has abandoned its 'white kit' for coloured clothes, and shorter versions of the game such as **Twenty20** have been played to accommodate TV schedules.
- Competition between television providers has been of great financial benefit to sport, especially to the Premier League football clubs; some satellite companies like Sky Television have specific sports channels and have developed the idea of 'pay to watch' for certain live fixtures.

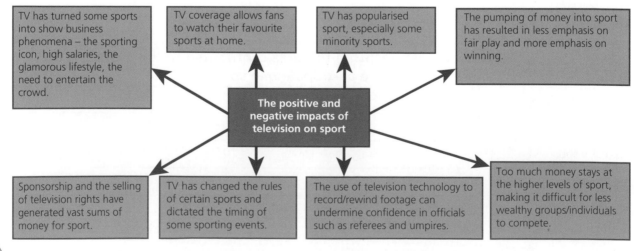

TV has turned some sports into show business phenomena – the sporting icon, high salaries, the glamorous lifestyle, the need to entertain the crowd.

TV coverage allows fans to watch their favourite sports at home.

TV has popularised sport, especially some minority sports.

The pumping of money into sport has resulted in less emphasis on fair play and more emphasis on winning.

The positive and negative impacts of television on sport

Sponsorship and the selling of television rights have generated vast sums of money for sport.

TV has changed the rules of certain sports and dictated the timing of some sporting events.

The use of television technology to record/rewind footage can undermine confidence in officials such as referees and umpires.

Too much money stays at the higher levels of sport, making it difficult for less wealthy groups/individuals to compete.

Sponsorship and its impact on the development of sport

Revised

Sponsorship has transformed modern sport. Companies want to be associated with sport because direct links with clubs and/or players will help promote their company name and sell their products. Commercial sponsorship now operates at professional and amateur levels and at national and local levels.

- In high profile sports, large sums of money are involved in sponsorship – the late 1990s saw the building of the Ricoh Arena in Coventry and Arsenal's Emirates stadium in London.
- **Sponsors** will have their logo displayed on sports kits, on banners at the event and on printed material linked to that event – companies like Flora have sponsored the London Marathon.
- Sports stars like David Beckham, Michael Owen, Lewis Hamilton and Gary Lineker have become wealthy through sponsorship and advertising.
- Most amateur sporting clubs and organisations could not survive without some form of sponsorship from local companies, who will sponsor kit, equipment and matches, and take out advertisements in match programmes.

Key terms

Sponsor – a person or business firm who pays all or some of the cost of putting on a sporting event

Sponsorship – financial support provided by a sponsor

Revision tasks

1. Copy out the table and use the information in this section to complete it.

Positive impact of television on sport	Negative impact of television on sport

2. Think of **four reasons** to support the statement 'Sponsorship has played a vital role in the development of sport in the late twentieth century.'

Controversy in sport

Sport used for political and propaganda purposes

Revised

Sport and sporting events have sometimes been used for political purposes. Here are some famous examples:

- **1936 Berlin Olympic Games:** Hitler attempted to use the Games for **propaganda** purposes to spell out the superiority of the Germanic Aryan race; his plan backfired as the black American athlete, Jesse Owens, won four gold medals and broke Olympic records; Hitler refused to attend the medal ceremony.
- **1968 Mexico Olympic Games:** the black American sprinters Tommie Smith and John Carlos used their medal ceremony to perform their black-gloved salute to the Black Power Movement, and to draw attention to racist attitudes within America.
- **1980 Moscow Olympic Games:** 64 countries, including the USA, boycotted the Games in protest over the Soviet invasion of Afghanistan the previous year.

Key term

Propaganda – attempting to persuade people to think and behave in a certain way

- **1984 Los Angeles Olympic Games:** in response to the Moscow boycott, fourteen Communist countries led by the USSR boycotted these Games.
- **1995 Rugby World Cup:** this was hosted by South Africa where President Mandela used the event to show the world that his country was making social and political progress following the ending of apartheid.

Terrorism and sport

Revised ☐

Terrorist organisations have used sporting events to make political statements:

- **1972 Munich Olympic Games:** the Palestinian terrorist organisation, Black September, raided the accommodation block holding Israeli athletes, killing two and taking nine others hostage. These hostages were later killed when the German authorities attempted a rescue mission, which also killed five terrorists.

Ever since the 1972 terrorist attacks there has been high security at all Olympic Games, as evident in the 2012 London Olympics.

Drug abuse in sport

Revised ☐

In their desire to be the best, to set records and to win medals, some athletes have used illegal drugs to improve their performance. This became a major concern during the late twentieth century following the suspicion that the East German authorities were forcing their athletes to use **performance enhancing drugs**. The country won nine gold medals in 1968, twenty in 1972 and forty in 1976.

The following are examples of athletes who have been found guilty of using performance enhancing drugs:

- 1988: the athlete Ben Johnson received a two-year ban for taking anabolic steroids.
- 1991: the footballer Diego Maradona received a 15-month ban for taking cocaine.
- 1999: the athlete Linford Christie received a two-year ban for taking nandrolone.
- 2003: the athlete Dwain Chambers received a two-year ban for taking tetrahydrogestrinone.
- 2003: the cricketer Shane Warne received a one-year ban for taking a banned diuretic.

Consequently, all athletes are now subject to regular drug testing and there have been calls for the punishments to be more severe.

> **Key term**
>
> **Performance enhancing drugs** – illegal substances used to improve sporting performance

> **Revision tasks**
>
> Use the information in this section to complete the following.
>
> 1. Give **three** examples of how sport has been used for political purposes.
> 2. Think of **three** reasons/examples to support the statement 'The last three decades have seen a sharp increase in the use of performance enhancing drugs by athletes.'

Chapter 5 The changing nature of popular entertainment in Wales and England

> ## Key issues
>
> You will need to demonstrate good knowledge and understanding of the key issues of this period:
>
> - What kinds of entertainment were influential in people's lives up to 1945?
> - What were the major developments in the 1950s and 1960s?
> - How has mass entertainment developed in recent times?

5.1 What kinds of entertainment were influential in people's lives up to 1945?

People's entertainment

Theatres and music halls

Revised ☐

By 1900 most towns had a theatre and a music hall. They were very popular forms of entertainment before the First World War:

- **Theatres** tended to attract middle-class crowds; the works of Gilbert and Sullivan, such as *HMS Pinafore* and *The Mikado*, were popular.
- **Music halls** were more popular with the working class. The audience would be encouraged to laugh and sing along with the entertainers; stars like Marie Lloyd and Harry Lauder were popular.

> **Key terms**
>
> **Theatre** – a building with a stage on which plays and other entertainments are performed
>
> **Music hall** – a theatre in which a variety of entertainments such as songs and comic turns take place

Social activities provided by churches and chapels

Revised ☐

Church and chapel attendance during the early twentieth century was strong, especially in Wales after the 1904–05 Religious Revival. While Sunday was the main day of worship, churches and chapels also offered a range of leisure activities throughout the week. These included the opportunity to take part in or be entertained by:

- choirs
- eisteddfodau
- brass bands
- Cymanfa Ganu
- drama groups
- sporting teams

> **Key terms**
>
> **Eisteddfod** – (singular form of eisteddfodau) a festival of Welsh culture and tradition
>
> **Cymanfa Ganu** – a hymn-singing festival

Choirs and brass bands were common forms of entertainment and in Wales the Cymanfa Ganu or singing festival was also very popular. Equally important were the local eisteddfodau, which held competitions in singing, dancing and reciting Welsh poetry and literature.

Pubs and institutes

As well as company and alcohol, pubs offered entertainment such as darts, cards, bridge, quiz nights and even sports. However, not everybody approved of such social entertainment and the **Temperance Movement** campaigned against the consumption of alcohol.

Working Men's Clubs or Institutes offered facilities such as billiard (pool) rooms, concert halls and libraries.

Key term

Temperance Movement – an organisation which was against alcohol consumption

Revision tasks

Copy out the table and use the information in this section to complete it.

Venue	Type of entertainment offered by this establishment
Theatre	
Music hall	
Church/chapel	
Pub	
Working Men's Institute	

The impact of the cinema

The popularity of the silent cinema

The first cinema in Britain opened in Balham in south London in 1907. In Wales, the first purpose-built cinema was the Carlton in Swansea, which opened in 1914. After the First World War, the cinema developed as a very popular form of entertainment, with most towns having a 'picture palace' by the 1920s. They showed short, silent, black and white films that were often accompanied by a pianist. Many early cinemas were hastily built 'flea pits' but, as they grew in popularity, they were replaced with grander buildings with names like The Empire, The Majestic, and The Scala. Popular films were slapstick comedies of Charlie Chaplin and Harold Lloyd, the romantic films of Rudolph Valentino or Ivor Novello, or the historical epics of Cecil B. de Mille.

Key term

Escapism – attempt to avoid reality by indulging in pleasurable fantasies

The reasons for the growth in popularity of the cinema

- The novelty of new technology, a moving picture, was appealing.
- It was another form of social entertainment.
- People saw the attraction of movie stars.
- The ticket prices were cheap.

- Films provided a form of **escapism**.
- People had more leisure time than before.
- There was usually a wide range of films on offer.
- From 1927 'talking' films ushered in a new phase of popularity.

The 'golden age' of cinema-going

The arrival of the first talking film in 1927 (*The Jazz Singer*, staring Al Jolson) added to the popularity of the cinema. By the 1930s over half of the UK population went to the cinema at least once a week. Stars like Clark Cable, Errol Flynn and Greta Garbo became household names and their new films were eagerly awaited.

By 1934 Wales had over 320 cinemas. A year later, the first Welsh language talkie, *Y Chwarelwr (The Quarryman)*, was a big hit in North Wales. The film *How Green Was My Valley* (1941) showed a romantic view of life in a coal-mining community in the South Wales valleys. In this interwar period cinema had a major impact on people's lives.

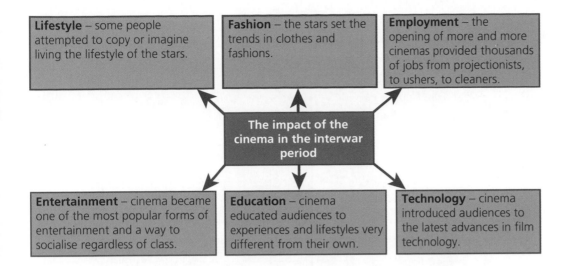

Lifestyle – some people attempted to copy or imagine living the lifestyle of the stars.

Fashion – the stars set the trends in clothes and fashions.

Employment – the opening of more and more cinemas provided thousands of jobs from projectionists, to ushers, to cleaners.

The impact of the cinema in the interwar period

Entertainment – cinema became one of the most popular forms of entertainment and a way to socialise regardless of class.

Education – cinema educated audiences to experiences and lifestyles very different from their own.

Technology – cinema introduced audiences to the latest advances in film technology.

The cinema during the Second World War

The cinema during the Second World War

Although all films were subject to censorship, the cinema played an important role during the Second World War:

- Keeping up morale – through short propaganda films displaying the fighting British spirit
- Providing an escape – distracting people's attention from the hardships of life on the Home Front
- Relaxation – relieving the tension and worry by providing a place to relax and socialise
- Providing information – showing short news reports before the main feature, as well as public

information films about air raid precautions and the **blackout**.

Key term

Blackout – the period in the Second World War when light from all windows had to be hidden so it could not be seen by enemy aircraft

Popular films included *The Way to the Stars* (1945) (about the RAF) and *Millions Like Us* (1943) (a propaganda film about life on the Home Front), and the American films *Gone With the Wind* (1939) and *Casablanca* (1942).

Revision task

Copy out the table and use the information in this section to complete it.

Reasons why the cinema became a popular form of entertainment	The impact the cinema had on the lives of ordinary people	The role of the cinema during the Second World War

The impact of the radio

The development of the radio during the 1920s and 1930s

Often referred to as the 'wireless', radio sets were mass produced during the 1920s. This made them affordable to many working-class people. The British Broadcasting Company (BBC) was set up in 1924, then renamed the British Broadcasting Corporation in 1927 to become a public company. It was paid for by issuing radio licences.

Number of radio licences issued, 1923–34	
1923	200,000
1929	2,600,000
1934	5,700,000

The radio became a major form of entertainment and had a significant impact on people's lives.

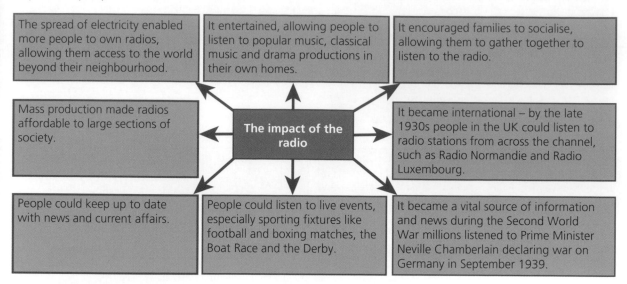

The spread of electricity enabled more people to own radios, allowing them access to the world beyond their neighbourhood.	It entertained, allowing people to listen to popular music, classical music and drama productions in their own homes.	It encouraged families to socialise, allowing them to gather together to listen to the radio.
Mass production made radios affordable to large sections of society.	**The impact of the radio**	It became international – by the late 1930s people in the UK could listen to radio stations from across the channel, such as Radio Normandie and Radio Luxembourg.
People could keep up to date with news and current affairs.	People could listen to live events, especially sporting fixtures like football and boxing matches, the Boat Race and the Derby.	It became a vital source of information and news during the Second World War millions listened to Prime Minister Neville Chamberlain declaring war on Germany in September 1939.

The role of the radio during the Second World War

Revised ☐

As with the cinema, the radio played a key role in keeping up morale during the war:

- The Ministry of Information controlled broadcasts, using censorship to deliver a positive message.
- The radio proved a vital source of news and information, although setbacks like the evacuation of British troops from Dunkirk in May–June 1940 were deliberately made to sound less serious than they really were.
- Millions listened to Prime Minister Winston Churchill's regular radio broadcasts about the course of the war.
- In 1940 the BBC started *The Forces Programme*, broadcasting dance music and variety shows to entertain the armed forces.
- To avoid the bombing in London, the BBC's Variety Department was moved to Bangor in North Wales in 1940; its most popular programme was *It's That Man Again* (*ITMA*) with comedian Tommy Handley.

Revision tasks

Use the information in this section to complete the following.

1. Identify five reasons why the radio became a popular form of entertainment during the 1920s and 1930s.

2. Rank these reasons into an order of importance, explaining the reasons for your rank order.

Exam practice

Describe the role of the radio in the Second World War. **[4 marks]**

Answers online

Exam tip

In 'describe' questions you need to demonstrate specific knowledge, covering two or three key factors. In this instance you need to spell out the radio's function as a source of popular entertainment and its more important role during the war years of providing information and news. You should mention that broadcasts were subject to censorship, and that they included political speeches as well as special programmes for the armed forces.

5.2 What were the major developments in the 1950s and 1960s?

The development of television and the cinema

One form of popular entertainment which saw dramatic growth in the 1950s was television:

- The BBC began television broadcasts in 1936 but very few people owned a television set before the 1950s.
- Due to the war, the BBC stopped its television broadcasts between 1939 and 1946.
- By the early 1950s television availability had spread across much of Britain; the first BBC transmitter station in South Wales was opened in 1952.
- The real boom in television ownership came as a result of the broadcast of the Coronation of Queen Elizabeth II in 1953, when over half of the UK population watched the event live.

- ITV (Independent Television) was launched in 1955 as a **commercial television** service to provide competition to the BBC; it is largely financed through advertising, unlike the BBC, which is funded through the TV licence fee.
- ITV controls the regional television companies, which have to compete to win the franchise for an area; HTV (Harlech TV) operated the franchise for Wales between 1968 and 2002.

> **Key term**
>
> **Commercial television** – television funded by advertising

- TV ownership continued to expand dramatically during the 1960s. By 1966 over 85 per cent of homes had a television.

Number of TV licences issued, 1962–68	
1962	12,000,000
1965	13,000,000
1968	16,000,000

- Television sets were expensive, so many people had to rent them.
- In 1964 a second BBC channel, BBC2, was launched; it concentrated on educational and cultural programmes.
- In 1966 over 33 million viewers watched England play in the final of the World Cup.
- Colour TV made its first appearance in 1967 but the BBC and ITV did not begin broadcasting in colour until 1969.

- TV programmes shut down before midnight, but on 20 July 1969 ITV made the first ever all-night broadcast to show the Apollo 11 moon landing.
- Several television programmes developed immense followings during the 1960s, having a dramatic impact on the nation's viewing habits:
  - The soap opera *Coronation Street* was first broadcast by Granada Television in 1960.
  - Comedies such as *Steptoe and Son* and *On the Buses* attracted huge audiences.
  - Children's programmes like *Blue Peter* and *Thunderbirds* began long-running careers.
  - Police dramas like *Dickson of Dock Green* and *Z Cars* were very popular.
  - Pop music shows like *Juke Box Jury* and *Top of the Pops* were popular among teenagers and young adults.
- In the days before video recording, programmes had to be watched when they were broadcast and this affected people's social lives.

The decline in cinema attendance

The cinema continued to be popular in the 1950s but attendance declined steadily during the 1960s, largely due to the growing influence of television:

- Hollywood feature films in colour continued to attract audiences in the 1950s, making household names of stars like Marilyn Monroe, Humphrey Bogart and John Wayne.
- By the late 1950s cinema audiences were in decline – an increase in entertainment tax caused ticket prices to rise and a lack of new investment caused many cinemas to become rundown.
- Many cinemas were forced to close down: there were 3000 cinemas in England and Wales in 1960 but only 1500 by 1969.

Revision task

Using the information in this section, give at least three reasons for each of the following:

1. The decline in cinema audiences during the 1950s and 1960s.

2. The growth in TV audiences during the 1950s and 1960s.

Exam practice

Why do Sources A and B have different views about the impact of television? **[8 marks]**

> **Source A:** Gerry George, a TV presenter and actor, recalling his memories of television on an Internet website (2010)
>
> 'The magic of television came into my home in 1951, when I was in my early teens. The arrival of that magic box transformed my life. Oh happy days! From then on, my whole life focused on that tiny "box of delights" and its memorable viewing. Thank you, television!'
>
> **Source B:** Tom Barrance, a media historian, writing in a GCSE history textbook, *Sport, Leisure and Tourism since 1900 (1998)*
>
> 'Since the 1950s, television has affected the lives of virtually everyone in Wales and England in some way. Some of the effects have been positive, but many have been negative. Some reports claim that television has had a bad effect on lifestyles as it stops families talking to each other; others say there is too much bad language and violence on television.'

Answers online

Exam tip

In this type of question you need to compare and contrast two sources, making clear reference to both the content and the authors. You need to provide a judgement about why the views differ and this can best be explained through the attributions – Source A is the memory of a retired TV presenter and actor, while Source B is written by a historian for educational purposes. Source A is biased; Source B offers a more balanced view.

The impact of popular music and the development of musical styles

From the 1950s onwards sales of **vinyl records** increased sharply. Popular music became an important influence.

Key term

Vinyl record – a circular plastic disc storing recorded music

The 1950s: Rock 'n' roll

At the end of the Second World War big bands dominated popular music, but by the mid-1950s a new form of music – **rock 'n' roll** – had arrived from America. It had a fast beat and relied on the guitar, bass and drums. Artists such as Elvis Presley, and Bill Haley and his Comets, became extremely popular, especially with younger people. Their parents were less enthusiastic and disapproved of the energetic style of dancing. **Skiffle**, an alternative style of music which also developed at this time, was inspired by artists like Lonnie Donegan.

Key terms

Rock 'n' roll – a form of popular music which originated in the USA in the 1950s, based on African-American rhythm and blues (R&B)

Skiffle – a type of popular music with jazz, blues, folk and roots influences, usually using homemade or improvised instruments. It became popular in the UK in the 1950s

Revised

- The Beatles from Liverpool changed the face of pop music in the 1960s by developing a new style based on harmony singing, guitars, bass guitars and drums. After their first single 'Love Me Do' reached number 17 in the charts in 1962, they followed it with a string of chart-topping singles. They became the first British group to break into the American music scene.

- Other British groups, such as the Rolling Stones, the Who, the Hollies and the Kinks, copied and developed the Beatles' style, becoming highly successful.

- The 1960s also saw the development of other styles of music:
  - the Californian surf music of the Beach Boys
  - the folk music of Bob Dylan
  - Motown, a style of soul music with a distinct pop influence, popularised by the Jackson Five and the Supremes
  - in Wales the Sain record label was founded to provide an outlet for Welsh language artists such as Dafydd Iwan
  - the Welsh singer Tom Jones, who emerged onto the pop scene in the mid-1960s, quickly becoming a bestselling vocalist

Key terms

Long-playing album – a vinyl record 12 inches (30cm) in diameter which contains a collection of songs

45 rpm single – a vinyl record 7 inches (18cm) in diameter with one song on each side which revolves around the turntable 45 times per minute

Discothèque – disco; a place where people dance to modern recorded music for entertainment; now called a nightclub

Investiture – the official presentation of a title

Evolution of the teenager – the 1960s saw the emergence of a 'generation gap' between teenagers and their parents; teenagers spent their money on records and related pop music material such as magazines, posters, badges and T-shirts.

Fashion – young people flocked to wear the same style of clothes as their pop idols, such as the leather jacket, the mini-skirt, the parka, the flowered shirt; they also copied their hairstyles.

The media – private radio stations such as Radio Caroline were set up to play pop music; in 1967 the BBC created Radio 1, a station dedicated to pop music; ITV launched its pop programme *Ready Steady Go* and the BBC responded with *Top of the Pops;* music magazines like *Melody Maker, Sounds* and the *New Musical Express* were launched.

The impact of pop music in the 1960s

Youth culture – separate youth cultures developed, each with their distinctive styles of music, dress and behaviour, with styles such as mods, rockers and hippies.

Technology – the 1960s saw the introduction of the **long-playing album (LP)** as an addition to the **45 rpm single;** the transistor radio, which could be run off batteries and was thus portable, was developed.

Clubs and concerts – open-air music festivals were held in Hyde Park, London, and on the Isle of Wight from 1968 to 1970; more and more people went to concerts to listen to live bands; by the late 1960s the **discothèque** was becoming popular.

Protest – pop music of the 1960s became linked to political protest; Bob Dylan and Joan Baez protested against the Vietnam War; Sam Cooke composed 'A Change is Gonna Come' about the fight for Civil Rights in the USA; in Wales Dafydd Iwan wrote 'Carlo', a Welsh language protest song against the **investiture** of Prince Charles in 1969.

Revision tasks

1. Copy out the table below and use your knowledge to complete each section.

Style of music	Period when this style first became popular	Key features of this style of music	Examples of musical artists representing this style
Rock 'n' roll			
Skiffle			
The Beatles			
Motown			

2. Explain the impact that each of these factors had on the development of pop music in the 1960s:

    Youth culture   Clubs and concerts   Radio   Political protest

5.3 How has mass entertainment developed in recent times?

The continuing appeal of pop music

Pop music continued to have great influence on entertainment and lifestyle after the 1960s, when new varieties of musical styles and new types of pop artists appeared.

Varieties of pop music in the 1970s

Revised ☐

The pop music styles of the 1970s included:

- **Glam rock**, also known as 'glitter rock', was performed by singers and musicians who wore outrageous clothes, make-up and hairstyles, particularly platform-soled boots and glitter; examples of this style are David Bowie, Marc Bolan, Elton John and the Sweet.
- **Punk rock** emerged in the mid-1970s and set out to shock people with its fast, loud music and **anti-establishment** lyrics; the media treated punks as a symptom of a broken society; examples of this music style are the Sex Pistols, the Clash and the Damned.

There were also different types of fans, such as the **teenybopper**, a young teenager, typically a girl, who became fanatical over pop stars like David Cassidy, Donny Osmond and the Bay City Rollers.

> **Key terms**
>
> **Glam rock** – a style of rock music of the 1970s associated with glittery and outrageous costumes
>
> **Punk rock** – a fast and aggressive music style of the late 1970s, often with offensive lyrics
>
> **Anti-establishment** – going against accepted authority
>
> **Teenybopper** – a fanatical young pop music fan of the 1970s

Varieties of pop music in the 1980s and 1990s

Revised ☐

- Pop music continued to grow and flourish into the 1980s. Synthesisers, drum machines and computerised keyboards came to dominate musical trends with groups like the Human League and Duran Duran rapidly growing in popularity.
- **Britpop** emerged in the early 1990s and was characterised by bands influenced by British guitar pop music of the 1960s and 1970s; examples of this style of music include Oasis and Blur.
- **Cool Cymru**: Welsh pop bands became very successful at the start of the new millennium, the best-known examples being the Stereophonics, the Manic Street Preachers and Catatonia.

> **Key terms**
>
> **Britpop** – a style of music of the 1990s which looked back on guitar pop music of the 1960s and 1970s
>
> **Cool Cymru** – a nickname for the Welsh musical scene in the late 1990s and early 2000s

Women in pop

Revised ☐

- Female singers like Cilla Black, Dusty Springfield and Mary Hopkins were very successful in the 1960s and 1970s.
- Female artists of the 1980s and 1990s had stronger, more independent images than their predecessors; Madonna was one of the bestselling artists of the 1980s; in the 1990s the Spice Girls became very popular, selling the image of **'Girl Power'**.
- In the 1990s Welsh singer-songwriter Cerys Matthews, former lead singer with Catatonia, helped popularise Welsh pop music.

> **Key term**
>
> **Girl Power** – an empowering phrase associated with the popularity of female pop groups of the late 1990s, also linked to consumerism

Pop on television

Revised

- Music shows remained very popular on TV with programmes like *Top of the Pops* and the *Old Grey Whistle Test* (on BBC2) attracting loyal audiences.
- The development of satellite and cable television resulted in the introduction of specific music channels like MTV.

- The music video became an essential tool in successfully marketing records, with bands competing for the best video; the rock group Queen produced many popular videos.
- The twenty-first century has seen the rise of music talent shows like *Pop Stars*, *Pop Idol*, *The X Factor* and *The Voice*.

Developments in music technology

Revised

The period from the 1970s has seen dramatic developments in the way people listen to music:

- In 1979 Sony introduced the **Walkman**, a portable machine with headphones which played cassette tapes; in the 1980s cassette sales overtook vinyl record sales.
- In 1982 **CD players** using digital laser technology were introduced; by the 1990s CD sales outstripped cassette and record sales.
- In the 2000s digital music using **digital audio players**, usually MP3 players or smartphones, has become the norm.

> **Key terms**
>
> **Walkman** – portable audio cassette player
>
> **CD player** – compact disc player that plays audio tracks
>
> **Digital audio player** – portable media device that stores and plays digital audio files

The music industry

Revised

The music industry consists of companies and individuals who make money by creating and selling music:

- The musicians who compose and perform the music
- The companies which create and sell recorded music – music publishers, producers, and recording studios like Universal and Sony

- Those who promote the music – booking agents and promoters
- Professionals who assist musicians and their music careers – managers and entertainment lawyers
- Those who broadcast music – TV, satellite, Internet and radio companies
- Those who write about the music scene – journalists and music magazines like *MOJO*, *The Fly*, *NME* and *Q Magazine*.

Pop concerts and good causes

Revised

Pop music has been increasingly used to support charitable and humanitarian causes:

- In the 1970s Rock against Racism and the Campaign for Nuclear Disarmament (CND) both held outdoor concerts in London to raise awareness of their causes.
- The 1980s saw the growth of large rock concerts for charity, which have continued to this day:
  - The 1985 Live Aid Concert raised millions for the Ethiopian famine relief.
  - In 2005 Tony Christie and Peter Kay raised money for Comic Relief through their cover of the song 'Is this the way to Amarillo?'
  - In 2010 over twenty artists came together to cover the song 'Everybody Hurts' to raise money for the Haiti earthquake appeal.

> **Revision tasks**
>
> The changes in popular music since the 1970s include:
>
> Different varieties of pop music
> The Walkman and CD player
> The music video
> Satellite and cable TV
> Rock concerts for charity and good causes
>
> Using your own knowledge and the information in this section, for **each** change above, a) describe what the change is and b) briefly explain how this change has helped the development of pop music.

Changes in television and film watching

Changes in television provision and viewing

Revised

The impact of television on people's lifestyles has continued to grow as the choice and range of programmes has expanded:

- 1982: Channel 4 was launched.
- 1982: S4C (*Sianel Pedwar Cymru*) was launched as a Welsh language television channel; its soap opera *Pobel y Cwm* started in 1988 (making it the longest-running soap opera in Europe after *Coronation Street*).
- 1983: breakfast TV was launched.
- 1989: satellite and cable networks were first made available; Sky Television quickly developed as a major supplier.
- 1997: Channel 5 was launched.
- 2008–10: the switch-over from analogue to digital TV signal took place, which provided viewers with a greater choice of programmes.

People now have a range of TV channels to watch, catering for all interests, such as 24-hour news, sport, documentaries, films, music and politics. The development of the video recorder in the 1980s, DVD recorders in the 1990s and now digital TV recorders have enabled people to record and watch programmes when they want.

> **Key term**
>
> **Couch potato** – a lazy person whose recreation consists chiefly of watching television and videos

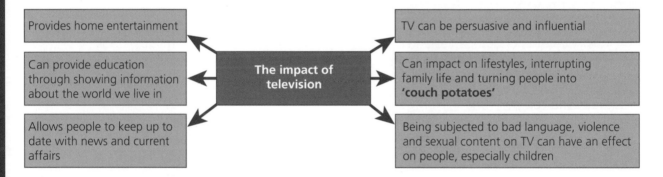

Provides home entertainment

Can provide education through showing information about the world we live in

Allows people to keep up to date with news and current affairs

The impact of television

TV can be persuasive and influential

Can impact on lifestyles, interrupting family life and turning people into **'couch potatoes'**

Being subjected to bad language, violence and sexual content on TV can have an effect on people, especially children

Changes in film viewing

Revised

- Cinema audiences continued to decline during the 1970s and 1980s.
- The growth of TV channels and the development of the video recorder provided more opportunities for people to watch films at home.
- In the 1990s film companies fought back with improved technology, special effects, stereo sound and 3D; films like *Jurassic Park* (1993) began to win back audiences.
- The introduction of multi-screen cinemas offered more choice and helped to start a revival in cinema audiences; 2009 had the best viewing figures since the late 1960s.

Developments in entertainment technology

Developments in radio entertainment

The radio has remained important in the lifestyle of the British people. The number of radio stations available has increased since the 1970s:

- 1973: introduction of commercial radio stations; one of the first was Capital Radio in London.
- 1974: Swansea Sound became the first commercial radio station in Wales.

- 1977: Radio Cymru became the first dedicated Welsh language channel.
- 1992: Classic FM became the first UK national commercial radio station.

Computers, interactive gaming and the Internet

The 1900s saw a massive growth in the sale of personal computers that offered opportunities for home entertainment:

- In the 1980s Nintendo introduced the first video game console, the NES, and in 1994 Sony launched its PlayStation. In 2001 Microsoft introduced the Xbox and more recently Nintendo the Wii.
- The Internet has had a dramatic impact on entertainment, providing instant communication via email, discussion forums and social networking sites such as Facebook.

Mobile phones and music players

The use of mobile phones has spread rapidly during the last two decades and phones have become more and more sophisticated. Smartphones now offer Internet connection, double up as digital music players and video cameras, and allow access to social networks.

Revision task

1. Copy out the table below and use the information in this section to complete it. Think of three factors for each column.

Positive impact of TV	Negative impact of TV

2. Explain the part played by each of the following in the development of entertainment:

   The radio   The computer   The mobile phone

Exam practice

There have been many developments in popular entertainment since 1900. Has television been the most important development in popular entertainment from 1900 to the present day?

[10 marks + 3 marks for SPaG]

Answers online

Exam tip

In the extended writing question you need to develop a balanced answer, supported by facts, that considers two sides of an argument. In this instance you need to comment on how television emerged as an important form of popular entertainment. You then need to discuss other important developments. Remember to end with a clear judgement.

Chapter 6 Changes in holiday patterns in Wales and England

Key issues

You will need to demonstrate good knowledge and understanding of the key issues of this period:

- What opportunities did people have for holidays up to 1950?
- How much did tourism and holiday patterns change in the 1950s and 1960s?
- How far have tourism and holiday patterns changed since the 1960s?

6.1 What opportunities did people have for holidays up to 1950?

Traditional holiday resorts

Seaside resorts   Revised

- The spread of the railway network during the second half of the nineteenth century helped people to access seaside resorts from major urban areas.
- The Bank Holiday Act (1871) gave workers an extra six days off a year.
- Annual paid holiday was still at the discretion of the employer but became more common.
- Seaside resorts became popular destinations for a new breed of 'tourist'; workers from London took the train to resorts on the south-east coast such as Southend, Brighton and Margate; workers from the Midlands were attracted to resorts on the coast of north-west England, such as Blackpool and Southport, or to resorts on the North Wales coast like Rhyl and Llandudno.
- Some resorts like Margate, Southport and Llandudno aimed to attract the professional classes, who tended to stay in large hotels with names like The Grand, The Imperial or The Regent.
- Less wealthy holidaymakers stayed in **guesthouses**; they brought their own food which the owner cooked for them.
- Popular activities within the resorts included bathing and paddling, donkey rides, Punch and Judy shows, strolling along the **promenade** or visiting the **pier**.

Key terms

Guesthouse – a private house in which rooms and meals are provided for paying guests

Promenade – a place for a leisurely walk along the sea front

Pier – a structure with a deck that is built out into the sea

How far does Source A support the view that seaside holidays were becoming popular in the early twentieth century?. **[5 marks]**

Source A: An advert for hotel accommodation in the seaside resort of Llandudno, North Wales, which appeared in a travel guide published in 1900

Answers online

Spa towns and inland resorts

Revised ☐

Many wealthy tourists visited **spa towns** which advertised the medicinal benefits of 'taking the waters'. It was claimed their mineral waters would benefit those suffering from illnesses such as gout, rheumatism and heart disease, and skin complaints such as eczema.

- Popular English spa towns included Bath, Buxton, Harrogate and Leamington Spa.
- Popular Welsh spa towns included Llandrindod Wells, Builth Wells and Llanwrtyd Wells.

The railway also helped to make inland resorts more accessible. The Lake District became popular, as did the mountain landscape of Snowdonia in North Wales. The Snowdon Mountain Railway opened in 1896.

Key term

Spa town – a town where water comes out of the ground and people come to drink it or lie in it because they think it will improve their health

Day excursions

Revised ☐

Many working-class people lacked the time or money to take long holidays, but they could take day trips which were often organised by the local church, chapel or club. They would travel either by train or by **charabanc**.

- For workers in the South Wales Valleys, a day trip to Barry Island or Porthcawl was popular.
- For workers from the Midlands, a daytrip by train to Rhyl or Prestatyn on the North Wales coast was popular.
- Alternatively, people could visit a local beauty spot.

Key term

Charabanc – a motorised coach used for sightseeing tours

Holidays abroad for the well-to-do

Revised

- During the eighteenth and nineteenth centuries it was fashionable for the upper classes to go on a '**Grand Tour**' of the Continent. This was seen as a formal way for a young rich man to complete his education.
- The spread of the railway in the second half of the nineteenth century made travel on the Continent much easier and more affordable for the middle classes.
- Monte Carlo, Venice and Switzerland became popular destinations by the turn of the twentieth century.
- Tour companies like Thomas Cook emerged to organise such holidays.
- The outbreak of war in 1914 did much to hinder continental travel.

Key term

Grand Tour – an extended tour through Europe by rich travellers, largely for educational purposes

Revision task

Use the information in this section to write two sentences to describe the type of holiday that was on offer, and the types of people who went on them, for each of the following headings:

Traditional seaside resort

Spa town

Day excursions

Holidays abroad

New developments in holiday patterns in the 1920s and 1930s

The 1920s and 1930s saw changes in holiday patterns in England and Wales. People increasingly saw short breaks and holidays as an important part of their lifestyle.

Time off and holiday pay

Revised

- By 1929, over 3 million workers received at least one week's holiday with pay.
- The Holiday with Pay Act (1938) made it a legal requirement for all employers to provide holidays with pay.
- Many industries developed annual holiday periods which saw companies shut down for a short period:
  - ○ In South Wales the **miners' week** saw a mass migration of workers to holiday resorts like Porthcawl and Barry.
  - ○ In the north of England the **wakes week** saw a migration of industrial workers to coastal resorts like Blackpool.

Key terms

Miners' week – an annual paid holiday for industrial workers in South Wales

Wakes week – an annual paid holiday for industrial workers in north-west England

Lido – an open-air swimming pool

Greater use of charabancs and private cars

Revised

Developments in road transport opened up new destinations and new kinds of holidays to tourists. Trains remained popular but the 1930s saw a growth in charabanc excursions, which provided day trips for thousands of workers. As car ownership increased (2 million cars on the road by 1939) people had more chance to explore the countryside. For the less wealthy, the motorbike provided a cheaper method of transport, and could be fitted with a sidecar to take a passenger.

Developments in seaside resorts

Revised

- Most holidaymakers still stayed in guesthouses, though these now became 'full board' (all meals included) or 'bed and breakfast' (offering accommodation and breakfast only); owners often had a reputation for being very strict.
- Many resorts attempted to upgrade by offering new facilities like a **lido**; Blackpool opened its lido in 1923 and many other resorts followed suit; bathing costumes were still all-in-one but they now showed arms and legs; health and fitness classes were offered, and beauty contests put on.
- Fish and chip shops, fairgrounds, dance halls and souvenir shops began to appear.

Hiking, cycling and camping holidays

Revised ☐

The 1930s saw developments in hiking and cycling breaks:

- The Youth Hostel Association was established in 1930; it provided cheap accommodation for hikers, cyclists and other visitors to the countryside; by 1939 it had over 300 hostels.
- The Ramblers Association was established in 1935 to promote walking for pleasure and to protect the rights of walkers (or ramblers).

- Cycling clubs, many of which had been formed in the early twentieth century, became popular in the 1930s; examples include the Leicestershire Road Club, the Warrington Road Club and Yorkshire Velo.
- Camping, a cheap form of holiday, also grew in popularity.

The development of holiday camps

Revised ☐

- The 1930s saw the development of the **holiday camp** as an affordable and popular holiday experience for the working class.
- In 1936 Billy Butlin set up his first holiday camp at Skegness in Lincolnshire; it cost £2 10s (£2.50) per person per week including all meals, activities and entertainment; Butlin's slogan was 'A week's holiday for a week's pay'.
- By 1939 there were nearly 200 holiday camps across England and Wales and over 500,000 people had visited them.

Key term

Holiday camp – a place, especially at the seaside, providing accommodation, meals and entertainment for holidaymakers

Revision task

Copy out the table below and use the information in this section to complete it.

Factor	How this changed holiday patterns in the 1920s and 1930s
Time off and 'holiday with pay'	
Charabancs and cars	
Changes to seaside resorts	
More active holidays	
Holiday camps	

Exam practice

Use the information in Source A and your own knowledge to explain why holiday camps became popular in the 1930s. **[4 marks]**

Source A: Taken from a school history textbook written in 2006

'Although leisure time and disposable income remained limited, the interest in travelling grew in the first half of the twentieth century. Coastal resorts like Brighton and Bournemouth became popular. In 1931, Harry Warner opened his first holiday camp on Hayling Island, followed by Billy Butlin at Skegness in 1936. Holidaymakers enjoyed accommodation in basic but bright chalets, three meals a day and entertainment for an all-inclusive price. These holidays grew in popularity.'

Exam tip

In this type of question you need to make use of what is said in the source and, most importantly, use your own knowledge to add extra information. In this instance the source says that many people did not have much money to spend on holidays in the 1930s, and the holiday camps offered accommodation, meals and entertainment. You could add that this new style of holiday was popular with families as it was more informal than the traditional accommodation, and offered an all-in-one package.

Answers online

6.2 How much did tourism and holiday patterns change in the 1950s and 1960s?

The high point of British holidays, 1945–65

During the Second World War, many beaches were mined and closed to the public. After the war the mines were cleared and the beaches re-opened. The 1950s saw more people taking an annual holiday. The period 1945–65 is usually regarded as the high point of the 'great British family holiday'.

The reasons for the growth in British holidays after 1945

Revised ☐

- People felt relief at the end of the war, which encouraged spending.
- There were better wages and improved living standards.
- More people were now entitled to holidays with pay.
- There was better road transport.
- Holiday camps such as Butlins and Pontins developed.
- Caravan holidays became increasingly popular.
- There was better advertising and sales of holidays.

Growth in caravan holidays

Revised ☐

- There was a sharp growth in the number of people taking caravan holidays after the Second World War.
- Caravans offered a cheap form of holiday and were affordable to the working classes.
- The number of caravan sites increased, particularly along coastal areas like Towyn in North Wales and Porthcawl in South Wales.
- Some caravan parks developed facilities such as social clubs, swimming pools and games rooms.
- Caravans provided independence, allowing their owners to tour the country.
- Many saw a short caravan break as an escape from home life.

The growth of the holiday camp

Revised ☐

- The 1950s and 1960s became the 'golden age' of the holiday camp.
- Many disused army camps after 1945 were converted for holidays.
- The holiday camp provided what holidaymakers were looking for – reasonably priced accommodation, plentiful food and a range of entertainment.
- In 1946 Fred Pontin opened his first holiday camp at Brean Sands near Burnham-on-Sea in Somerset.
- By 1949 he had opened six. They differed from Butlins camps in that they were smaller.
- Butlins continued to expand, with ten camps built between 1936 and 1966; camps were opened at Bogner Regis (1960), Minehead (1962) and Barry Island (1966).
- While such camps attracted thousands of visitors, they were criticised for being too structured; the 'Redcoat' entertainers in the Butlins camps directed all activities.

The impact of the motor car

Revised

- Improved wages after the war meant more people could afford to own a car.
- In 1939 2.5 million cars were registered in the UK; by 1963 this had grown to 7.5 million (one in four families now owned a car).
- The **'Beeching Axe'** of 1963 brought about the closure of 5000 miles (8000 km) of railway line and resulted in increased car usage.
- Seaside resorts had to adapt to cater for tourists with cars; hotels and guesthouses had to have car parks; roadside cafes opened; **motels** began to appear.
- The first 'Little Chef' roadside restaurant opened in 1958; others quickly followed along A roads and motorways.
- More and more people took to the road for 'daytrips'.
- This growth in car ownership had some negative impacts:
  - It caused overcrowded roads, especially in towns and resorts.
  - Some routes to the coast became clogged with traffic during the holiday season.
  - More roads such as bypasses and ring roads had to be built to tackle the congestion.

> **Key terms**
>
> **'Beeching Axe'** – the closing of many railway lines in the 1960s
>
> **Motel** – a roadside hotel for motorists

The need for National Parks

Revised

In 1949 the National Parks and Access to the Countryside Act was passed. It had two aims:

- to conserve the natural beauty, wildlife and cultural heritage of a specified area
- to promote opportunities for public enjoyment within that area.

> **Key term**
>
> **National Park** – an area of great natural beauty protected by law

During the 1950s ten **National Parks** were set up:

Country	National Park	Year created
England	Peak District	1951
	Lake District	1951
	Dartmoor	1951
	North York Moors	1952
	Yorkshire Dales	1954
	Exmoor	1954
	Northumberland	1956
Wales	Snowdonia	1951
	Pembrokeshire Coast	1952
	Brecon Beacons	1957

The growth in car ownership made many Parks within easy reach of holidaymakers and day trippers. The Parks promoted tourism by offering a range of activities including:

- walking
- climbing
- cycling
- horse-riding / pony-trekking
- watersports (sailing, canoeing)
- wildlife watching.

Examples of two popular National Parks:

Snowdonia	• Largest National Park in Wales, covering 823 square miles (2130 km²) • Home to 26,000 people • Contains picturesque villages such as Betws y Coed and Beddgelert as well as mountainous scenery • An area rich in Welsh culture and history
Lake District	• Most visited National Park, with 15 million annual visitors and 23 million annual day visits • Largest of the National Parks in England • Includes 16 lakes, the largest of which is Lake Windermere

Exam practice

Explain why National Parks were set up in the 1950s. **[5 marks]**

Answers online

Exam tip

In 'explain why' questions you need to give two or more reasons and support your answer with specific factual detail. In this instance you need to talk about the desire to protect the local environment and provide access to stunning and unspoilt scenery. You could also mention it was hoped the Parks would promote rural tourism and offer a range of holiday experiences.

Revision task

Use the information in this section to create a spider diagram with 'Changes in holiday patterns and tourism during the 1950s and 1960s' in the middle. Arrange these four factors around it:

Caravan holidays

Holiday camps

The motor car

National Parks

Add your own notes, explaining how each factor helped to bring about the changes.

6.3 How far have tourism and holiday patterns changed since the 1960s?

The increasing use of air travel

During the 1960s, changes in tastes and expectations caused a shift away from traditional family holiday destinations in the UK to destinations abroad.

Package holidays and foreign destinations

Revised

From the late 1960s cheaper air travel made holidays in the Mediterranean more affordable. Mediterranean resorts offered a warmer climate and guaranteed sunshine:

- Travel companies began to offer **package holidays** which included airfare costs and accommodation in the total price.
- Pontins took advantage of this new craze: 'Pontinental Holidays' offered all-inclusive holidays in Sardinia, Majorca, Spain and Ibiza.
- By the 1970s large stretches of the coast of southern Europe had become geared to **mass tourism**.
- By 1979 10 million British people took a holiday abroad; over 50 per cent booked a package tour.

Key terms

Package holiday – a holiday arranged by a travel company in which travel and accommodation are booked for you

Mass tourism – when lots of people go on holiday to the same place at the same time

Long-haul flights and cheaper airfares

Revised

- In 1979 Sir Freddie Laker launched his no-frills 'Skytrain' air service, offering cheap flights to the USA.
- During the 1980s destinations outside Europe were becoming affordable. The USA emerged as a popular destination.
- Laker Airways went bankrupt in 1982 but it laid the foundations for other low-budget airlines such as Ryanair (1984), Virgin Atlantic (1984) and easyJet (1995).
- These low-budget airlines have helped to make flights affordable and enabled more people to holiday abroad.

The impact of the package holiday

Revised

- Holidays abroad have led to lifestyle changes at home – people began to experiment with foreign cooking at home and there are now more restaurants offering cuisine from around the world.
- Clothing began to change – more sunhats and shorts.
- Tourists came home with souvenirs of their holiday abroad.
- Many Spanish resorts became 'mini-Englands', with pubs, fish and chip shops and English beer readily available.
- UK resorts were forced to adapt quickly to fight to keep hold of tourists in the face of stiff competition from package holidays.

The British holiday fights back

Updating traditional resorts and developing a tourist industry

Revised

- Holiday camps suffered from the rise in package holidays and came to be seen as outdated and old-fashioned.
- Butlins attempted to rebrand itself in the 1980s by developing 'themed worlds': Somerwest World in Minehead (1986), Funcoast World in Skegness (1987) and Starcoast World in Pwllheli (1990).
- Upmarket versions of holiday camps began to appear, concentrating on outdoor activities such as cycling and walking but also with indoor water complexes. Center Parcs first opened in 1987 and had four UK locations by 1997; Bluestone in Pembrokeshire opened in 2008 and contains the Oakwood Theme Park.
- Seaside resorts built large leisure complexes with indoor beaches, wave machines and tropical climates; for example, Swansea Leisure Centre attracted 750,000 visitors a year during the 1990s.
- Beach resorts have attempted to clean up their environment – the Blue Flag scheme has improved the quality of beaches.
- The National Parks have used adverts to attract visitors – towns like Windermere in the Lake District are packaged to attract walkers, horse-riders and lovers of outdoor pursuits.

The development of new tourist attractions

To encourage people to holiday in Britain, the tourist industry has developed a range of new attractions.

Theme parks

Revised ☐

These offer daring rides and activities. Parks compete against each other to offer more adventurous rides. Some of the top **theme parks** include:

- **Alton Towers (Staffordshire):** a 'Disneylike' park with themed areas and a range of rides
- **Drayton Manor (Staffordshire):** featuring some of the biggest and scariest rides
- **Thorpe Park (Surrey):** with the world's first horror movie themed rollercoaster
- **Legoland (Berkshire):** featuring themed rides, Lego model cities and landmarks
- **Blackpool Pleasure Beach (Lancashire):** with 125 rides, including Europe's tallest rollercoaster

> **Key term**
>
> **Theme park** – a leisure attraction that focuses on exciting rides and events

Country parks and nature trails

Revised ☐

Local authorities have set up **country parks** to encourage people to explore the countryside near them, as well as **nature trails**, woodland walks and cycle trails:

- Millennium Coastal Park at Llanelli
- Loggerheads Country Park outside Mold in North Wales

> **Key terms**
>
> **Country park** – an area of countryside set aside for public recreation
>
> **Nature trail** – a path through the countryside to draw attention to nature features

Heritage centres and museums

Revised ☐

In recent decades, heritage sites offering a 'journey into the past' have become very popular:

- **St Fagans (Cardiff):** an open-air museum outside Cardiff which contains over 40 original buildings moved from sites across Wales and reconstructed in the museum; it also contains displays of traditional Welsh crafts and cultural heritage items.
- **Ironbridge (Shropshire):** a collection of museums, including an open-air reconstructed Victorian town with buildings relating to the Industrial Revolution.
- **Beamish (County Durham):** an open-air museum of buildings from the Victorian and Edwardian eras.

Organisations like the National Trust hold special events when historical re-enactment societies put on displays or guides dress in period costume.

Copy out the table below and use the information in this section to complete it.

Feature	This has changed holiday patterns since the 1960s by ...
Package holidays	
Low-budget airlines	
New types of UK holiday venues	
Theme parks	
Heritage museums	

Continuity and change in modern holidays

Modern trends in holiday patterns

Revised ☐

Trends in holidays continue to change but it is also possible to detect some continuity:

- About 75 per cent of holidays taken by British people in 2012 were spent in Britain, a figure which matched that of 1970.

- About 25 per cent of British people holidayed abroad in 2012; in earlier decades, the holidays tended to last longer and cost more.

- In comparison with 1970, people in 2012 had more leisure time, increased income and higher standards of living.

- Holiday destinations have changed, with certain 'hot spots' developing at particular times: in the 1970s and 1980s Majorca and Ibiza were extremely popular; in more recent times cities like Prague, Barcelona and Amsterdam are popular for short breaks.

- Sophisticated advertising and competition between travel firms to sell holidays, together with the growth of the Internet, have made it easier for people to book flights, hotels and excursions.

- Holiday companies have also begun to target specific groups:
  - Club 18–30 offers cut-price holidays for young men and women.
  - Saga targets the traveller aged 50 upwards.

Multi-holidays

During recent decades it has become increasingly popular for people to have more than one holiday a year, for example winter breaks or long weekends as well as a summer holiday:

● In 1971, 15 per cent of UK residents had more than one holiday a year; in 1986, 21 per cent; and in 2001, 29 per cent.

Environmental concerns

Concerns over the environmental impact of travel are now beginning to be recognised by the holiday industry. There are attempts to reduce the **carbon footprint** of tourism. Aircraft manufacturing companies are trying to build more fuel-efficient planes to reduce CO_2 emissions. Hotels try to encourage guests not to request clean towels and bed linen every day of their stay. Some holidays advertise their eco-friendly qualities by offering locally sourced food, or using solar energy or woodchip burners. This area is evolving.

Key term

Carbon footprint – the amount of carbon emissions created by people through day-to-day activities

Revision task

Identify **three** ways in which holiday patterns have changed in the last two decades.

Exam practice

How important have theme parks been to the development of the British tourist industry? **[6 marks]**

Answers online

Exam tip

In the 'how important/successful' questions you need to identify two to three key reasons for why something was important/successful, using specific factual detail to back up your comments. In this instance you should refer to how theme parks offer an exciting alternative holiday experience, and how they complete with each other. This helps keep the British holiday industry alive and allows it to fight back against the appeal of overseas holidays. Remember to provide a judgement on 'importance'.

Chapter 7 Changing crimes and their causes in Wales and England

Key issues

You will need to demonstrate good knowledge and understanding of the key issues of this period:

- What were the main causes and types of crime, 1530–1700?
- How did types of crime and their causes change, 1700–1900?
- Why have there been new causes and types of crime from 1900 to today?

7.1 What were the main causes and types of crime, 1530–1700?

Crime during the sixteenth and seventeenth centuries	
Continuity Minor crime like petty theft remained the most common (74% of all crime) and violent crime also continued (around 15%)	**Change** The appearance of specific crimes associated with **vagrancy, heresy** and **treason**

Key terms

Vagrancy – wandering from place to place without a settled home or job

Heresy – beliefs which went against the teachings of the Church

Treason – plotting against the monarchy and/or government

The problem of poverty

There was a sharp rise in poverty during the sixteenth century, caused by a number of factors.

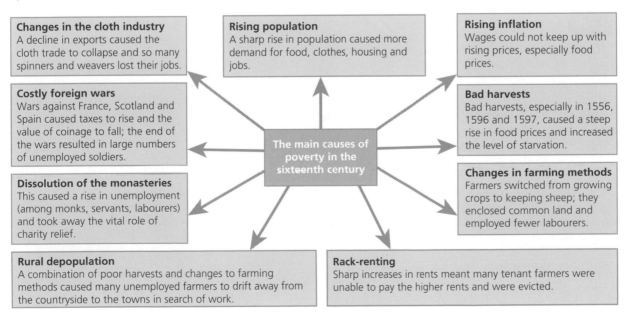

Changes in the cloth industry
A decline in exports caused the cloth trade to collapse and so many spinners and weavers lost their jobs.

Rising population
A sharp rise in population caused more demand for food, clothes, housing and jobs.

Rising inflation
Wages could not keep up with rising prices, especially food prices.

Costly foreign wars
Wars against France, Scotland and Spain caused taxes to rise and the value of coinage to fall; the end of the wars resulted in large numbers of unemployed soldiers.

Bad harvests
Bad harvests, especially in 1556, 1596 and 1597, caused a steep rise in food prices and increased the level of starvation.

The main causes of poverty in the sixteenth century

Dissolution of the monasteries
This caused a rise in unemployment (among monks, servants, labourers) and took away the vital role of charity relief.

Changes in farming methods
Farmers switched from growing crops to keeping sheep; they enclosed common land and employed fewer labourers.

Rural depopulation
A combination of poor harvests and changes to farming methods caused many unemployed farmers to drift away from the countryside to the towns in search of work.

Rack-renting
Sharp increases in rents meant many tenant farmers were unable to pay the higher rents and were evicted.

Different sorts of vagabonds

Revised

A Tudor JP (Justice of the Peace), Thomas Harrison, classified **vagabonds** and **rogues** according to the activities they specialised in. The most common types were:

- **Angler:** used a hook on the end of a long wooden stick to steal clothes/valuables.
- **Clapper dudgeon:** used arsenic on their skin to make it bleed, hoping to attract sympathy while begging.
- **Doxy:** stole chickens by feeding them bread tied to a hook; carried stolen goods in a large sack on their back.
- **Counterfeit crank:** dressed in tatty clothes and pretended to have fits, sucking soap to fake foaming at the mouth.
- **Abraham man:** pretended to be mad.

Key terms

Vagabond – wandering beggar who often turned to crime

Rogue – a dishonest person; a wandering beggar who turned to crime

The rising number of vagabonds during Elizabethan times

Revised

The rising number of vagabonds, especially during the reign of Elizabeth I, caused people to feel threatened and worried by the increase in crime. This fear was based on several factors:

- Vagabonds were seen to be idle and too lazy to find a job.
- They were too prepared to turn to crime as a way of life.
- By wandering from place to place they helped to spread disease, especially the plague.
- They increased the fear of rebellion, especially as many vagabonds were ex-soldiers.
- The burden of looking after the poor was increasing, causing **poor rates** to rise and fuelling resentment from those having to pay for this relief.

Key term

Poor rate – a tax raised in each parish to pay for the relief of the poor

Elizabeth's government attempted to reform the system of poor relief by passing the Elizabethan Poor Laws of 1598 and 1601, which punished lazy vagabonds and made each parish responsible for looking after its poor.

Revision task

Copy out the table and use the information in this section to complete it.

Reasons for the increase in vagabonds	Problems caused by the increase in vagabonds	What was done to tackle the problems caused by vagabonds

The crime of heresy

Revised

During the early sixteenth century, the German monk Martin Luther criticised bad practices and abuses within the **Roman Catholic** Church. This resulted in the Protestant Reformation and the birth of the **Protestant** faith. Religious disputes came to dominate the reigns of the Tudor monarchs, as the official religion of England and Wales switched between the Roman Catholic and Protestant faiths. Those people who refused to follow the 'official' religion were accused of being **heretics**. Heresy was a crime punishable by death:

- During the reign of Mary I (1553–58) 280 heretics were put to death for refusing to give up their Protestant faith; this compared with two people who died for their Catholic faith during the reign of Edward VI and four during Elizabeth's reign.

- In Wales, three Protestants were put to death during Mary's reign: Robert Ferrar, Bishop of St David's, at Carmarthen; Rawlins White, a fisherman, at Cardiff; and William Nichol, a labourer, at Haverfordwest.

Heretics were burned at the stake because it was believed they had rebelled against God. Some people believed that it was necessary to burn the body to free the soul and allow it to ascend to Heaven. Others believed burning was necessary to destroy all remains and leave nothing for Judgement Day, when God would resurrect Christian believers.

Key terms

Roman Catholic – Christians whose religious leader is the Pope; they believe the Pope to be God's representative on Earth with greater authority than a monarch

Protestant – Christians who reject the authority of the Pope and most of the Catholic Church's teachings and ceremonies

Heretic – a person whose religious views go against the officially approved belief

---

Henry VIII: Roman Catholic
- Ruled 1509–47
- King replaces Pope as Head of the Church
- Church services and prayers remain in Latin
- Priests not allowed to marry

Edward VI: Protestant
- Ruled 1547–53
- King is Head of the Church
- Church services and prayers in English (New Prayer Book)
- Priests could marry

The religious helter skelter under the Tudor monarchs

Elizabeth I: Protestant
- Ruled 1558–1603
- Queen becomes 'Governor' of the Church
- Church services and prayers in English
- Priests could marry

Mary I: Roman Catholic
- Ruled 1553–58
- Pope is Head of the Church
- Church services and prayers in Latin (New Prayer Book banned)
- Priests had to separate from their wives

Opposition to religious change during the Tudor period

Revised

People who strongly believed in their faith found it hard to accept the swings in religion under the Tudor monarchs. Of those who disagreed:

- some went into exile abroad
- others were willing to die for what they believed in
- others learned to keep quiet and pretended to conform.

Pilgrimage of Grace, 1536
Led by the lawyer Robert Aske, this was a religious protest involving 30,000 pilgrims protesting about changes made to the Church by Henry VIII. During October 1536 they took control of York, Hull, Pontefract and Doncaster. Henry sent troops to crush the rebellion. 178 protestors were executed, including Aske.

Protest from individuals
Protestant Bishops Latimer and Ridley were burnt at the stake in 1555 during the reign of Mary I for refusing to turn Catholic. In Wales, Richard Gwyn was put to death in Wrexham in 1584 during the reign of Elizabeth I for spreading Catholic ideas.

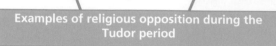

Examples of religious opposition during the Tudor period

Catholic printing press in the secret cave at Rhiwledyn
William Davies, a Catholic priest, was executed at Beaumaris in 1593. He was accused of helping to publish Catholic literature using a secret printing press in a cave at Rhiwledyn on the Little Orme, Llandudno.

John Penry, a Welsh Puritan martyr
Penry, a Puritan, disliked Elizabeth's religious settlement. During 1588–89 he became involved with a secret printing press which was used to spread Puritan ideas. He was eventually arrested, put on trial and found guilty of treason for his attacks on the Church. He was executed in May 1593.

Revision task

From the information in this section, give at least three reasons/examples for each of these:

- Reasons for the growth of heresy during the Tudor period
- Reasons for the harsh punishment given to heretics
- Examples of religious opposition during the Tudor period

Key terms

Puritan – an extreme type of Protestant who wanted a simple service and plain church

Treason – displaying disloyalty to the monarch or government

The crime of treason

Revised

During the sixteenth century treason was punishable by death, usually by being hung, drawn and quartered. Following his break with Rome, Henry VIII created himself Head of the Church in England. To protect his new position he issued a revised Treason Law in 1534. The clauses of this Act meant that political as well as religious opinions could now be classed as treasonable:

- Anyone who said or wrote things against the King, his wife or his heirs, or who displayed support for the Pope, was guilty of treason.
- Anyone who said the beliefs of the King went against the teachings of the Church, or said that the King was using his power unjustly, was guilty of treason.
- Anyone who kept silent when questioned on what were the rights and authority of the King was guilty of treason.

During the reign of Elizabeth I the Treason Law was extended to include anyone who said she was not the rightful Queen.

The threat posed by acts of treason

Revised

The Tudor and Stuart monarchs were constantly looking out for possible rebellions and plots that might challenge their authority and position. The reasons for such threats could be religious, political or economic, and were often a combination of these.

Key term

Gallows – wooden frame from which the hanging noose is attached

The Wyatt Rebellion, 1554

A Protestant nobleman, Sir Thomas Wyatt, led a force of 4000 protestors from Kent on a march to London. He planned to overthrow Mary (Catholic) and replace her with Elizabeth (Protestant) as Queen. He was defeated and executed for treason, together with 90 rebels.

Teenage Apprentice Riots, 1595

Some starving teenage apprentices in Southwark, London, in June 1595, were arrested and punished for stealing food. This led to riots across the capital. The disturbances ended when five rioters were hanged from the gallows for treason.

Examples of treasonable disturbances during the Tudor and Stuart period

The Monmouth Rebellion, 1685

This was an attempt by James, Duke of Monmouth and the illegitimate son of Charles II, to overthrow his uncle, the Catholic ruler James II. The rebellion failed. Monmouth and 331 rebels were executed for treason, and 849 rebels were sent overseas as slaves.

The Popish Plot, 1678

Titus Oates, a priest, made up the story of a plot to kill Charles II and replace him as king with his Catholic brother, James. Thirty-five men were executed for treason before Oates was arrested and sent to prison for perjury (making false statements under oath).

The threat posed by the Gunpowder Plot, 1605

Revised

One of the most serious acts of treason during this period was the Gunpowder Plot of November 1605, a religiously motivated attempt by a group of Catholic gentlemen to assassinate King James I.

> **Key term**
>
> **Recusant** – a person, usually a Roman Catholic, who refused to attend church services

Reasons for the plot

Many Catholics were angry that King James had enforced laws against Catholic worship. They disliked the heavy fines imposed on recusants for not attending Church of England services. Some Catholics were fined or imprisoned for taking part in Catholic services, and Catholic priests were accused of treason for trying to convert people to Catholicism.

The plan

- Led by Robert Catesby, the plotters planned to blow up the King during the state opening of Parliament.
- A cellar was rented underneath the House of Lords.
- Guy Fawkes, an ex-soldier, had the job of smuggling in and storing 36 barrels of gunpowder.
- Fawkes was also responsible for setting the fuse.

The failure of the plan

- One of the plotters sent a letter to the Catholic Lord Mounteagle, warning him not to attend the opening of Parliament.
- Mounteagle showed the letter to the King.
- During the night of 4 November guards arrested Fawkes in the cellar.
- Fawkes was tortured and the other plotters were eventually tracked down.

The consequences

- The plotters who survived capture were put on trial and found guilty of treason.
- In January 1606 they were publicly executed by being hung, drawn and quartered.
- The harshness of the punishment was intended to put others off the idea of committing treason.
- There is a theory that the King's Chief Minister, Robert Cecil, knew about the plot beforehand but allowed it to develop to discredit the Catholics.
- The plot served to make the Catholics unpopular and enabled harsher laws to be passed against them.

Exam practice

Describe the crime of treason in the sixteenth and seventeenth centuries. **[4 marks]**

Answers online

Exam tip

When answering 'describe' questions you need to ensure that you include two to three key factors. To obtain maximum marks you need to support them with specific factual detail, in this instance defining the crime of treason and providing examples of treasonable acts during this period, such as the Gunpowder Plot.

7.2 How did types of crime and their causes change, 1700–1900?

Crime during the eighteenth and nineteenth centuries	
Continuity Minor crime remained the most common (74% of all crime) and violent crime continued (10%)	**Change** The appearance of specific crimes associated with smuggling, highway robbery and the impact of industrialisation

The 'golden age' of smuggling

Revised ☐

As society changed, the government was forced to introduce new laws and categorise new criminal offences which had not existed before, such as **smuggling**. The eighteenth century has been called the 'golden age' of smuggling.

> **Key term**
>
> **Smuggling** – the secret trade of goods in a deliberate attempt to avoid paying customs duties

Reasons for the increase in smuggling during the eighteenth century

Revised ☐

- **The cost of war:** to pay the expense of fighting costly foreign wars against France, the government had to increase taxes, especially customs and excise duties.
- **Excise duty:** traditionally this covered chocolate, tea, beer, cider and spirits, but after 1688 it was widened to include salt, leather and soap.
- **Customs duty:** customs duties kept on rising and were bitterly resented.
- **Black market:** with a 70 per cent tax on goods like tea, people were more than willing to buy cheaper smuggled goods.
- **Insufficient policing:** there were not enough customs officers to patrol the thousands of miles of British coastline.
- **Investors and venturers:** there were many venturers willing to invest money to finance smuggling in the hope of rich profits.
- **Social crime:** many people did not view smuggling as a 'real' crime.

> **Key terms**
>
> **Excise duty** – a tax imposed on goods made and consumed within a country
>
> **Customs duty** – a tax imposed on exported or imported goods
>
> **Black market** – when goods are sold and bought illegally, often avoiding paying tax
>
> **Venturer** – Someone who risks investing money in the smuggling of goods

The organisation of smuggling

Revised ☐

Smuggling made criminals considerable amounts of money. Large gangs like the Hawkhurst and Hadleigh gangs, which operated along the south coast of England, dealt with several cargo loads of smuggled goods each week. Each gang employed between 50 and 100 individuals, each performing a specific task: venturer (the investor); spotsman (responsible for directing the ship to shore); lander (arranged the unloading of the smuggled cargo); tubsman (carried the goods); and batsman (protected the tubsman).

Notable Welsh smugglers	
William Owen	• Operated a smuggling gang along Cardigan Bay and the Llŷn Peninsula during the 1720s and 1730s, supplying smuggled brandy and salt from his base in the Isle of Man • He was executed in 1747
Siôn Cwilt	• Operated a smuggling gang along the Ceredigion coast, storing smuggled goods in sea-caves • Wore a distinctive coat of colourful patches
Lucas family	• Operated a smuggling gang from Salt House on the Gower Peninsula • Hid smuggled goods in a cave at Culver Hole

The role of the customs and excise men

Revised

Despite laws designed to limit smuggling (such as the Hovering Act 1718 and the Act of Indemnity 1736), it was difficult to control the illegal trade.

- **Preventative Officers** who were part of the Customs and Excise Service were responsible for preventing smuggling activity and capturing those engaged in it.
- The coastline of England and Wales was divided into 33 areas with teams of Preventative Officers being spaced at regular distances.
- With so many people involved in smuggling, and with too few Preventative Officers, it was impossible to prevent all incidents.
- Even when smugglers were caught it was difficult to secure a conviction; witnesses were too scared to come forward and the smuggling gangs used threats and intimidation to protect themselves.

> **Key term**
>
> **Preventative Officers** – men employed by the Customs and Excise Department to police the smuggling trade

The decline of smuggling in the early nineteenth century

Revised

Changes in the law, rather than successful policing, caused an eventual decline in smuggling.

- In 1784 the duty on tea was cut from 119 per cent to 12.5 per cent, making tea an unprofitable cargo for smugglers.
- Reductions in duties on other items in the early nineteenth century helped reduce smuggling.
- The Napoleonic Wars (1804–15) led to the building of watchtowers along the south-east coast of England, which made it harder for smuggling gangs to operate.
- The establishment of the Coast Guard in the 1820s added a further hindrance.

> **Revision task**
>
> Copy out the table and use the information in this section to complete it.
>
> | The 'golden age' of smuggling | | | |
> |---|---|---|---|
> | Reasons for the rise in smuggling during the 18th century | Key people involved in the organisation of smuggling gangs | Key people involved in the policing of smuggling activity | Reasons for the decline in smuggling during the 19th century |
> | | | | |

The rise and fall of highway robbery

Reasons for the growth in highway robbery

Revised

Highway **robbery** took place in the sixteenth and seventeenth centuries but became more common in the eighteenth century. There were several reasons for this:

- Unpoliced roads offered opportunities for robbers to strike.
- Handguns became easier to obtain and use.
- Improved roads enabled more people to travel by **stagecoach**.
- The building of more coaching inns encouraged travel.

> **Key terms**
>
> **Robbery** – stealing using violence or the threat of it
>
> **Stagecoach** – a four-wheeled horse-drawn carriage used to carry passengers

- People were becoming wealthier and carried more money and jewellery.
- Limited banking facilities meant people had to carry cash.

Highway robbery – what it involved

Revised

- **Footpads** tended to rob pedestrian travellers; their attacks were often quite brutal.
- **Highway robbers** tended to attack stagecoaches and travellers on horses; such robberies often involved the use of firearms.
- Most highwaymen operated in pairs or small groups.
- The roads leading in and out of London, which lacked any means of law enforcement, were common venues for such robberies, e.g. near Hounslow Heath and Finchley Common.

Key terms

Footpad – a criminal who carried out highway robbery on foot

Highway robber – a criminal who carried out highway robbery mounted on a horse

Famous highway robbers	
Richard ('Dick') Turpin (1706–39)	• During the mid-1730s he operated with his partner Tom King on the Cambridge Road. • In May 1737 Turpin accidentally shot King during an attack. • He fled to Yorkshire, and in 1739 he was arrested for horse stealing and hanged at York.
William Page (1730–58)	• He operated on several roads radiating from London. • He was eventually captured in 1758 and hanged in Maidstone.
John Rann (1750–74)	• He operated on the Hounslow Road. • He was arrested six times for highway robbery but each court case against him collapsed. • He robbed a chaplain near Brentford in 1774 and was hanged soon after at Tyburn.

Reasons for the decline in highway robbery

Revised

By the early nineteenth century, attacks on the highway had become much less common and they had virtually ceased by the 1830s. Several factors contributed to this decline:

- The rapid growth of London filled in open spaces like Hounslow Heath, making ambushes more difficult.
- John Fielding set up the Bow Street Horse Patrol in 1763 to experiment with policing the roads of London; in 1805 a new patrol of 54 officers policed the roads leaving the capital.
- The spread of **tollgates** made it more difficult for highwaymen to make a quick getaway.
- JPs refused to license taverns which were the known haunts of highwaymen.

Revision task

Use the information in this section to complete the following.

1. Explain why highway robbery was a problem during the eighteenth century.
2. Name a famous highway robber and outline his criminal career.

The impact of industrialisation on crime

Revised

During the late eighteenth and early nineteenth centuries, industrial development caused people to migrate from the countryside to the rapidly expanding towns, looking for work in the new factories and mines. This process of **industrialisation** and **urbanisation** brought dramatic changes in how people lived and worked.

Key terms

Tollgate – a gate across a toll road at which travellers must stop and pay a fee to use the road

Industrialisation – the development of industry on a large scale

Urbanisation – the rapid growth of, and migration to, towns and cities

Factors which contributed to the growth of industrial towns

Revised

- **Changes in agriculture:** the introduction of new machinery resulted in less demand for rural labour.
- **Development of the factory system:** factories were **labour-intensive**; workers had to live close by.
- **Stable employment:** unlike agriculture, factory work was not seasonal; it offered employment to the whole family; wages were higher than those of agricultural labourers.
- **Improved transport:** development of the railways made travelling easier and cheaper.
- **Multiplier effect:** once one member of a family had migrated and found work, others soon followed.

Reasons for the sharp increase in crime in the nineteenth century

Revised

- **Population increase:** the UK population rose from 16 million in 1800 to 42 million in 1900.
- **Growth in the size of industrial towns and cities:** Manchester's population rose from 75,000 in 1801 to 303,000 in 1851; Merthyr Tydfil's population grew from 7705 to 46,378 during the same period.
- **Living and working conditions:** poor quality housing and squalid, unsanitary living conditions were ideal breeding grounds for crime to develop; there was a heavy concentration of people living in a small area and no security.
- **Economic problems:** the ending of the Napoleonic Wars in 1815 caused an increase in unemployment and poverty, which coincided with a period of bad harvests and high food prices.
- **Political unrest:** working-class individuals held protests demanding political, economic and social changes.

Development of the Victorian 'criminal class'

Revised

The nineteenth-century writer Henry Mayhew identified a 'criminal class' of people who survived through criminal activities. They tended to live in **rookeries** such as St Giles in London and they acquired nicknames depending on the crimes they specialised in:

- **Thimble-screwers:** they stole pocket-watches from their chains.
- **Prop-nailers:** they stole pins and brooches from women.
- **Drag-sneaks:** they stole goods or luggage from carts and coaches.

> **Key terms**
>
> **Labour-Intensive** – industries that need a lot of workers
>
> **Rookery** – overcrowded slum housing occupied by poor people, and often by criminals and prostitutes

Popular protest and crime during the nineteenth century

Revised

Between 1790 and 1840, economic and social hardship, combined with demands for political reform, resulted in a real threat of revolution. At times, the anger of protesters resulted in outbreaks of violence and criminal activity:

Luddism	1812–13	Attacks on factory machines in northern England, with handloom weavers protesting over new factory-based machine-woven cloth
Swing Riots	1830–31	Attacks by agricultural labourers on the property of rich farmers across south-eastern England; they set fire to hayricks and smashed machines; they were angry about their poverty and the introduction of farm machinery
Rebecca Riots	1839–43	Gangs of poor farmers disguised as women to hide their identity attacked tollgates in south-west Wales; they were angry about increased rents, **tithe** payments and tolls

> **Key terms**
>
> **Luddism** – the beliefs of textile workers who opposed the introduction of machines in new factories and took part in riots to smash up the machinery
>
> **Tithe** – a tax paid by farmers of one-tenth of their produce/income

Answers online

Revision task

Explain how each of the following factors contributed to the growth of crime during the nineteenth century:

Industrialisation   Poor living conditions
Development of a criminal class   Protests and riots

Exam tip

In the 'how important' questions you need to identify two to three key reasons for why something was important, using specific detail to back up your comments. In this instance you should refer to the sudden increase in population in the new towns, the overcrowded slum housing, the squalor and poor living standards; and even the resentment against the new factories, which caused attacks on the new machines.

Exam practice

How important was the growth of large industrial towns in causing new types of crimes in the early nineteenth century?   **[8 marks]**

7.3 Why have there been new causes and types of crime from 1900 to today?

Crime during the twentieth and twenty-first centuries	
Continuity Minor crimes such as petty theft, together with violent crimes such as robbery, assault and murder, continued little changed from previous centuries	**Change** The appearance of specific crimes such as transport crime; the trend towards violent crimes such as hooliganism and terrorism; and some new crimes which resulted from developments in technology, such as computer crimes

Crime figures have risen sharply since 1900 but much of this increase is associated with the increased reporting and recording of crime, improved policing methods and the improved use of scientific technology to detect crime.

The rise of transport crime   Revised

The 1920s saw the beginnings of **mass production** in the car industry. Between 1924 and 1936, car prices fell by over 50 per cent, which made them affordable to the middle classes. This increase in the number of cars on the road led to new laws for regulating motorised transport.

Key terms

Mass production –the manufacture of goods on a large scale using a standardised mechanical process

Breathalyser – machine that tests blood alcohol levels in a motorist's breath

Important road traffic legislation	
1930	Compulsory motor insurance brought in
1934	30 m.p.h speed limit introduced
1935	New compulsory driving test
1956	Yellow lines introduced to restrict parking
1967	**Breathalyser** introduced to help reduce drink-driving offences
1977	70 m.p.h. speed limit introduced on dual carriageways and 60 m.p.h. on single carriageways
1991	Law of 'causing death by driving under the influence of alcohol and drugs' introduced
2003	Law banning the use of hand-held mobile phones while driving introduced

Revision task

Give **three** reasons to explain the rise in transport crime since the 1920s.

Motoring offences have now grown into one of the biggest categories of crime and involve people from all social classes.

Common motoring offences/crimes	
Road traffic offences	Dangerous and careless driving; parking violations; speeding; car theft; **road rage; joyriding; car-jacking**
Documentation offences	Driving without a driving licence; no car insurance; no vehicle tax; no **MOT**
Accidents	Failing to stop after an accident; failing to report an accident
Alcohol/drug-related offences	Driving while being over the legal limit for alcohol consumption; refusing to give a roadside breath test; refusing to supply specimens for analysis
In-car safety violations	Not wearing a seatbelt; using a hand-held mobile phone while driving

The rise of computer crime

Revised ☐

Dramatic advances in computing technology have provided criminals with new opportunities for crime. While many of these types of **cybercrime** are new, others are simply new versions of old crimes.

Examples of cybercrimes	
Hacking	Gaining unauthorised access to the private records of individuals, organisations or governments
Spam	Sending bulk emails for commercial purposes
Phishing scams	Using spoof emails to trick people into revealing important information, for instance, an email that looks like it is from your bank and asks for your account details
Fraud and identity theft	Stealing a person's identity and pretending to be somebody else; stealing money from bank accounts via the Internet
Copyright infringement	Illegally downloading music and film; other forms of criminal piracy
Malicious software	Deliberately introducing a computer virus to damage or destroy information held on other computers
Sexual crimes	Child grooming through the use of chatrooms and social networks; the sharing of illegal images of children; harassment through sharing images without consent
Cyberbullying	Repeated threatening and hostile behaviour through Internet and smartphone use to intimidate and hurt another person

The trend towards violent crime

The growth of terrorism

Revised ☐

Britain has lived with the fear of **terrorist** activity since the 1960s. Terrorists use a range of methods to push their political demands. These have included hijackings, assassinations, taking hostages, bombings, suicide attacks and arson attacks.

In Britain the most serious threat has come from the **IRA**. Between 1969 and 2001 over 3526 people were killed in terrorist violence in Northern Ireland and on the British mainland:

● In October 1984 a bomb exploded in the Grand Hotel in Brighton in an attempt to blow up members of the British Cabinet.

● In June 1996 an IRA bomb exploded in the Arndale Shopping Centre in Manchester, injuring 212 people.

In Wales several nationalist groups fighting for a more independent Wales have carried out terrorist acts:

- Mudiad Amdduffyn Cymru or MAC (Movement for the Defence of Wales) was active between 1963 and 1969. MAC activists bombed official government buildings in Cardiff and pipes carrying water to Liverpool.
- Meibian Glyndŵr (Sons of Glyndŵr) carried out arson attacks on English-owned holiday homes in Wales between 1979 and 1994.

Internationally, terrorist groups like the **PLO** and the Baader Meinhof gang were active during the late twentieth century. More recently groups like **al-Qaeda** have been responsible for terrorist attacks such as the 9/11 attacks on 11 September 2001 on the World Trade Center in New York. Some of these groups have operated within the UK:

- The Pan AM Flight 103 was blown up over Lockerbie, Scotland, in December 1988, an event thought to be the work of Libyan terrorists linked to the regime of Colonel Gaddafi.
- The 7/7 attacks on 7 July 2005 involved a series of co-ordinated suicide bomb attacks on London's public transport network which were linked to al-Qaeda.

> **Key terms**
>
> **PLO** – the Palestine Liberation Organisation, formed to protect and represent Palestinians and to establish an independent Palestinian state
>
> **Al-Qaeda** – a global militant Islamist organisation founded by Osama bin Laden in 1989

Football hooliganism

Revised

Hooligans are often members of gangs, like belonging to a tribe, and violence is accepted as the norm. Football hooliganism occurred throughout the twentieth century but became a particular problem from the 1970s onwards:

- It often involved gangs of rival supporters fighting each other or attacking property.
- In 1985 fighting between British and Italian fans caused a wall to collapse in the Heysel Stadium in Belgium, killing 38 people.

In 1998 a Special Police Unit was set up to deal with football crime. It became the UK Football Policing Unit in 2005. Rival fans are now kept apart in grounds, seats have replaced stands, and banning orders have been used. Police now use CCTV, mounted officers and even helicopters to monitor football crowds.

> **Key term**
>
> **Hooligan** – a person who acts in a violent way and causes damage, often without thinking

Drug-related crime

Revised

Drug trafficking became more prominent during the late twentieth century. Planes, boats, trucks and people (**mules**) are used by gangs to smuggle illegal drugs into the UK. Drug gangs operate on their own 'turf' and use violence to protect their patch from rival gangs. All of this has increased gun and knife crime. Drug addiction has resulted in the increase of certain crimes such as burglary, mugging and robbery.

> **Key term**
>
> **Mule (drug trafficking)** – a person who agrees to carry illegal drugs into another country in return for payment

Gun and knife crime

Revised

As well as being associated with drug gangs, gun and knife crime is often linked to juvenile gangs. Gang members carry knives and sometimes guns as protection. Gun crime in England and Wales increased by 90 per cent between 1999 and 2009. In 2008 there were 277 deaths from stabbings in England and Wales.

> **Revision task**
>
> Define cybercrime, terrorism, hooliganism, drug-related crime, and gun and knife crime.

Chapter 8 Changing methods used to combat crime in Wales and England

Key issues

You will need to demonstrate good knowledge and understanding of the key issues of this period:

- How were law and order enforced, 1530–1700?
- What were the main turning points in policing methods, 1700–1900?
- How have policing methods developed from 1900 to today?

8.1 How were law and order enforced, 1530–1700?

Law enforcement during the sixteenth and seventeenth centuries	
Continuity The officers responsible for keeping the peace during the sixteenth and seventeenth centuries – the Justice of the Peace (JP), the Parish Constable and the Town Watchman – were the same as those that had existed at the end of the medieval period	**Change** An increase in the workload of the Justice of the Peace and the Parish Constable, and at the end of the seventeenth century the introduction of paid nightwatchmen (Charleys)

Justices of the Peace (JPs)

The role of the Justices of the Peace
Revised

The task of maintaining day-to-day law and order during the sixteenth and seventeenth centuries lay in the hands of unpaid, amateur officials. The most important law enforcement officer at local government level was the Justice of the Peace (JP), a post originating in medieval times. JPs were chosen from local landowners, whose social standing enabled them to command obedience through respect not force.

The duties of the Justice of the Peace
Revised

- **Maintaining law and order:** there were about twenty JPs per county. Their main role was to act as a magistrate and administer justice. Minor crimes such as petty theft, drunkenness and fighting were dealt with in the **Petty Sessions**. More serious cases such as murder, assault, witchcraft, **poaching** and rioting were dealt with in the **Quarter Sessions**. JPs had to pass on the most serious crimes to a judge and jury in the Assize Court. JPs also carried out policing duties, organising the Parish Constable and the Town Watchman in the maintenance of law and order.
- **Administering local government:** JPs were responsible for enforcing local government legislation such as licensing and regulating ale houses, checking weights and measures, and organising road and bridge repair. They also kept an eye on vagabonds, supervised poor relief and later administered the Elizabethan Poor Laws (1598 and 1601) and managed the new **houses of correction**.

> **Key terms**
>
> **Petty Sessions** – local courts at which two or more JPs would sit to deal with minor criminal cases so as not to overwhelm the Quarter Sessions
>
> **Quarter Sessions** – courts held every three months by JPs
>
> **Poaching** – illegally hunting animals, birds or fish on someone else's property
>
> **House of correction** – a prison for beggars who refused to work

- **Carrying out orders of the Privy Council and Council of the Marches:** JPs were expected to ensure that the Acts passed by the Privy Council and the Council of the Marches were enforced and obeyed, and issue appropriate punishments if not.

The effectiveness of Tudor Justices of the Peace

Revised

During the Tudor period the JPs' workload substantially increased, both in the towns, which were expanding, and in the countryside, where they had to deal with the growing problem of vagrancy. On the whole:

- they were effective in maintaining law and order at the local level
- as unpaid volunteers they performed a vital service in policing and punishing offenders
- their social standing enabled them to command respect and people acted on their decisions
- they were effective in ensuring Acts of Parliament were locally enforced.

JPs were only appointed for a year at a time and re-election depended on doing a good job. However, a small number did abuse their position and gained financially through their role as JP.

Revision task

Using the information in this section, answer the following:

1. What type of people became JPs?
2. What were the main duties of a JP?
3. How effective were JPs at law enforcement?

The role of Parish Constables and Town Watchmen

Revised

The maintenance of law and order depended on community self-policing. The **hue and cry** still operated but the main policing duties were undertaken by the Parish Constable and the Town Watchman, posts which had their origins in medieval times.

The JP appointed the Parish Constable from tradesmen or husbandsmen (farmers) living in the area. They held the unpaid post for one year and were expected to do this job as well as their day job. For many it was an unwanted burden and some wealthy individuals paid others to occupy the position instead of them. They did not have a uniform and or carry weapons.

Key term

Hue and cry – an alarm was raised when a crime had been committed and all citizens within earshot had to join the hunt for the suspect

The duties of the Parish Constable

Revised

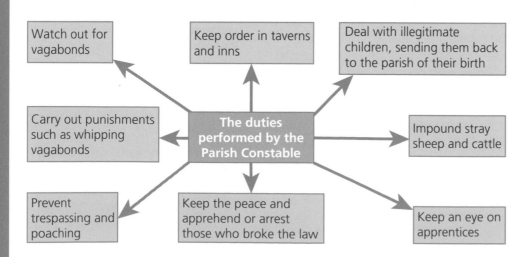

Watch out for vagabonds

Keep order in taverns and inns

Deal with illegitimate children, sending them back to the parish of their birth

Carry out punishments such as whipping vagabonds

The duties performed by the Parish Constable

Impound stray sheep and cattle

Prevent trespassing and poaching

Keep the peace and apprehend or arrest those who broke the law

Keep an eye on apprentices

The Town Watchman

Revised

The Town Watchman or **Bellman** was expected to patrol the streets at night and hand over any suspected wrongdoers to the Constable. They did not wear a uniform but dressed in thick heavy clothing and carried a bell, a lantern and a staff. Their presence was meant to deter thieves and reassure the townsfolk.

> **Key term**
>
> **Bellman** – a man who rang a bell, like a town crier

The Charleys

Revised

An Act of Council issued by King Charles II in 1663 created a force of paid nightwatchmen nicknamed 'Charleys'. Their job was to patrol the streets and look out for anything suspicious, but the poor pay meant that many were discouraged from doing the job well. Charleys quickly became objects of fun, and were often thought to hide away from trouble.

The effectiveness of Parish Constables, Town Watchmen and Charleys

Revised

As they were the only law enforcement officers at the local level, the Constable, Watchman and Charley played an important role in maintaining law and order. However, they were not always the best person to do the job:

- The unpaid posts of Parish Constable and Town Watchman were generally unpopular among those selected to serve, especially as the duties had to be performed alongside their existing day jobs.
- Few could afford the time to perform their duties in a thorough fashion.
- Charleys tended to be old or lazy to perform their duties well.

> **Revision task**
>
> Copy out the table below, using the information in this section to complete it.
>
> | Law enforcement officer | Types of jobs they were expected to perform | How effective were they in maintaining law and order? |
> | --- | --- | --- |
> | Parish Constable | | |
> | Town Watchman | | |
> | Charley | | |

8.2 What were the main turning points in policing methods, 1700–1900?

Law enforcement during the eighteenth and nineteenth centuries	
Continuity Maintaining law and order continued to be the responsibility of unpaid and untrained local officials – the JP, Constable and Watchman	**Change** Experiments in using a force of paid and trained officers based at Bow Street; the development of the Metropolitan Police Force and the development of police forces across the rest of the country

The emergence of thief-takers

Revised

The sharp rise in population levels, together with the growth of towns and cities, during the eighteenth and nineteenth centuries put great pressure on the medieval system of using unpaid amateurs to maintain law and order. One result of this was that some private individuals, known as thief-takers, started acting as unofficial policemen. They captured criminals and claimed the reward money, or acted as go-betweens and negotiated the return of stolen property for a fee.

Here are two noted thief-takers:

- **Charles Hitchen (c.1675–1727):** he was a **fence** and abused his position as Under City Marshall for London to put pressure on thieves to sell their goods through him; he would then negotiate a fee for the return of the stolen goods to their original owner.
- **Jonathan Wild (1683–1725), 'Thief-Taker General of Great Britain and Ireland':** having previously worked for Hitchen, Wild built up an empire of organised crime; he planned thefts, trained and organised burglars, and then negotiated the return of the stolen goods; he periodically turned in thieves to the authorities and so appeared to 'police' the streets of London.

> **Key term**
>
> **Fence** – a person who buys and sells stolen goods

The first experiments in policing: the work of Thomas de Veil

Revised

In 1729 de Veil was appointed JP in Bow Street near Covent Garden, an area of London with a high crime rate. He was active in going out with his constables to investigate crimes, making arrests and then passing judgement on the criminals in his court.

Henry Fielding and the Bow Street Runners

Revised

In 1748 Henry Fielding was appointed Chief Magistrate at Bow Street. In 1751 he published *An Enquiry into the Late Increase of Robbers etc*. Claiming that the system of using unpaid part-time constables was not working, he set up a force of six law officers who were paid, full time and well trained. Henry's motto for success in catching criminals was 'Quick notice and sudden pursuit'. He placed adverts in newspapers asking people to help him.

Sir John Fielding continues the work of the Bow Street Runners

Revised

Following Henry's death in 1754 his blind half-brother, John Fielding, continued the work of the Runners, extending and enhancing the policing of London's streets:

- In 1763 he secured a government grant of £600 to establish the Bow Street Horse Patrol to deal with highway robbery; it was so successful in cutting crime that the funding was stopped (though the highwaymen soon returned!); the Patrol was not re-introduced until 1805 following Patrick Colquhoun's campaign.

- In 1772 he established a newspaper, *The Quarterly Pursuit,* which was published four times a year and contained lists of crimes and descriptions of wanted criminals.
- In 1786 the newspaper was renamed *The Public Hue and Cry* and it now appeared weekly; in the early 1800s it became the *Police Gazette* and it marked the beginnings of a national crime information network.

Knighted in 1761, for his services in cutting crime in the capital, 'Sir' John continued to work at Bow Street until his death in 1780.

Patrick Colquhoun and the extension of the work of the Bow Street Runners

Revised

Other JPs continued the work of the Fielding brothers after their deaths. One of the most important JPs was Patrick Colquhoun.

- In 1792 the Middlesex Justices Act extended the Bow Street scheme by funding seven JPs in other parts of London, each of whom had six full-time 'Runners' under their command.
- In 1798, after a campaign by Colquhoun, the Thames River Police was established.
- By 1800 London was patrolled by 68 'Runners'.
- In 1805 a Horse Patrol of 54 officers armed with swords, truncheons and pistols was set up to patrol the highways around London; they were nicknamed 'Robin Redbreasts'.

By 1829, London had 450 constables and 4000 watchmen to police a population of 1.5 million.

The importance of these early experiments in policing

Revised

- The Runners introduced the idea of 'preventative policing' by attempting to stop crime from being committed, rather than dealing with the consequences of crime.
- Such experiments did lower crime levels in London and they did serve as a deterrent.

Exam practice

Why were the Bow Street Runners a turning point in methods of policing in the late eighteenth century? **[8 marks]**

Answers online

Revision task

Using the information in this section, explain what each of the following individuals did to improve policing methods:

Jonathan Wild	Thomas de Veil
Henry Fielding	John Fielding
Patrick Colquhoun	

Exam tip

This type of question on 'turning-points' requires you to spell out why a particular event resulted in change. In this case you need to refer to the failure of the inherited medieval system of using unpaid amateur constables and watchmen, and how Fielding's force of paid, full-time and well-trained officers was a large improvement, as was his use of newspapers to record details.

The establishment of the Metropolitan Police, 1829

Opposition to the idea of a police force

Revised

Establishing a formal, national police force was not a smooth path of development. It was more one of haphazard growth. In the early nineteenth century there was fierce opposition to it. Some believed that such a force would:

- limit individual freedom and liberty by allowing the government to interfere
- give the police too much power which they could use to limit the rights of individuals
- be very expensive and cause taxes to rise.

Robert Peel and the Metropolitan Police Act (1829)

In 1829 Robert Peel, the Home Secretary, was successful in getting Parliament to pass the Metropolitan Police Act. He argued that London needed a force of paid, full-time law officers who would investigate crimes, patrol the streets and prevent crime, and apprehend criminals.

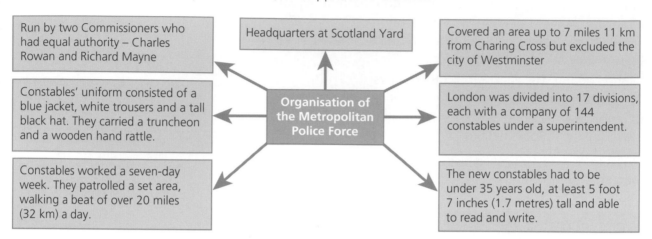

Run by two Commissioners who had equal authority – Charles Rowan and Richard Mayne

Constables' uniform consisted of a blue jacket, white trousers and a tall black hat. They carried a truncheon and a wooden hand rattle.

Constables worked a seven-day week. They patrolled a set area, walking a beat of over 20 miles (32 km) a day.

Headquarters at Scotland Yard

Organisation of the Metropolitan Police Force

Covered an area up to 7 miles 11 km from Charing Cross but excluded the city of Westminster

London was divided into 17 divisions, each with a company of 144 constables under a superintendent.

The new constables had to be under 35 years old, at least 5 foot 7 inches (1.7 metres) tall and able to read and write.

A second Metropolitan Police Act in 1839 extended the area to cover a 15-mile (24 km) radius from Charing Cross. This new police force proved to be effective in reducing crime rates, so was expanded. New specialist units were introduced over the following decades.

Later developments of the Metropolitan Police Force	
1852	Force to be headed by just one Commissioner
1862	Force strength had grown to 7,800 men
1882	Force strength had grown to 11,700 men
1890	Headquarters moved to New Scotland Yard
1900	Force strength had grown to 16,000 men, organised into 21 divisions

The extension of the police force outside London

Through a series of Acts of Parliament, the model of the Metropolitan Police Force was extended across the rest of the country.

Extension of the police force outside London	
Municipal Corporations Act (1835)	This allowed borough towns, if they wished, to set up a police force; only a small number (93 out of 171 boroughs) had done so by 1837.
Rural Police Act (1839) (or, County Police Act)	This allowed JPs to establish police forces in their county; only a small number (25 out of 55 counties) had done so by 1856.
County and Borough Police Act (1856)	This made it compulsory for every county to have a police force. Inspectors of Constabulary were appointed to report on the efficiency of each force.

To begin with the public were suspicious about these new police forces. There was widespread resentment over the running costs involved. It took some time for this suspicion and hostility to subside.

The beginnings of police specialisation

As the force developed its own specialist units to help with the detection of crime, its success rate in apprehending criminals improved, and this helped to make the police better accepted as part of the community.

Specialisms included the following:

- **The Detective Branch (1842):** these detectives dressed in civilian clothes to avoid being noticed by criminals.
- **The Criminal Records Office (1869):** this was set up in Scotland Yard. It compiled records of criminals from across the country.
- **The Criminal Investigation Department (1878):** known as the CID, this replaced the Detective Branch in investigating crimes.
- **The Special Irish Branch 1884:** initially set up to deal with Irish terrorism, it became the Special Branch in 1888.
- **Photography (1850s onwards):** provided visual images of criminals which could be circulated across the country.
- **Fingerprinting (1901):** developed by Sir Edward Henry, fingerprinting provided a unique record of individual identity.

> **Revision task**
>
> Using the information in this section, explain the part played by each of the following in the development of the police force in the nineteenth century:
>
> Metropolitan Police Act
> Municipal Corporations Act
> Rural Police Act
> County and Borough Police Act

8.3 How have policing methods developed from 1900 to today?

Law enforcement during the twentieth and twenty-first centuries	
Continuity The role of the police officer remained the same, the principal aim being the maintenance of public order and the prevention rather than the investigation of crime	**Change** Tremendous advances in forensic science; the use of computer technology to investigate crime; the development of specialist units to deal with particular aspects of crime investigation; and changes in transport

Increased resources for the police

Developments in transport

Revised

One of the biggest changes in policing during the first half of the twentieth century was due to new methods of transport:

> **Key term**
>
> **Bobby** – nickname for a policeman; after Sir Robert Peel

- 1909 – the first use of bicycles
- 1919 – introduction of police cars (not commonly used until the 1930s)
- 1930s – police motorbikes greatly improved police speed and effectiveness
- 1970s – 'bobby on the beat' replaced by patrol cars and 'rapid response' teams
- 1980s – introduction of police helicopters and light aircraft.

Developments in communications and technology

Revised

- **Telegraph and radio:** wireless communication was first used to enable the arrest of Dr Crippen in 1910; police telephone boxes appeared in the 1920s; two-way radios made their first appearance in the 1930s and are now an essential tool in modern policing.
- **Camera and video technology:** in 1901 the first police photographer was employed to record images of criminals; today photographs and video recordings play a vital part in any crime scene investigation; many police cars and all helicopters are fitted with cameras; the police also make use of **CCTV**.
- **Computer technology:** the Police National Computer came into use in 1974; today it holds databases for fingerprints, **DNA** records, motor vehicle records and missing persons.

> **Key terms**
>
> **CCTV** – closed-circuit television used for surveillance
>
> **DNA** – deoxyribonucleic acid, present in all living things and provides a unique genetic code or make-up for each individual body

Developments in police recruitment and training

Revised

The National Police Training College was set up in 1947 to provide new recruits with fourteen weeks of basic training and training courses for promotion; in 2012 the College of Policing took over responsibility for all police training needs.

The changing role and status of women police officers

Revised

Policewomen first appeared in 1919 but they had only limited duties such as patrol work, looking after children and female prisoners, and hospital duties. It was not until 1973 that they were granted equal opportunities to take on the same roles as male officers. In 1995 Pauline Clare became the first female appointed Chief Constable (for Lancashire).

The specialisation of police services

> **Revision task**
>
> Use the information in this section to help you describe the key developments in policing in each of the following areas:
>
> Communications and technology
>
> Policewomen   Transport

The development of specialist branches

Revised

Specialist unit and year founded	Principal function in the twentieth century
Criminal Investigation Department (CID) (1878)	Plainclothes detectives investigate major crimes such as murders, serious assaults, robberies, fraud and sexual offences
Flying Squad (1919)	Deals with serious theft; later became the Central Robbery Squad
Fraud Squad (1946)	Investigates fraud and other economic crimes
Dog Handling Squad (1946)	Trained officers use dogs to help trace people, property, drugs and explosives
Anti-Terrorist Branch (1971) (SO13)	Aims to monitor and prevent terrorist activity
National Hi-Tech Crime Team (2002)	Deals with serious and organised cybercrime
Counter Terrorist Command (2006) (SO15)	Formed from merger of Anti-Terrorist Branch (SO13) and Special Branch (SO12); it aims to prevent terrorist-related activity

Developments in forensic science

Revised

- **Fingerprinting:** following its first use in 1901, a national register of fingerprints was set up; in 1995 the National Automatic Fingerprint Identification System was introduced.

- **Forensic scientists:** Scenes of Crime Officers (SOCOs) attend crime scenes to examine and gather forensic evidence; they carry out tests on hair, skin, dust, fibres from clothing and traces of blood to match them to a suspect.

- **DNA and genetic fingerprinting:** since the 1980s police have increasingly depended on DNA and **genetic fingerprinting** to help solve crimes and investigate past, unresolved crimes; a DNA National Database was established in 1995.

> **Key term**
>
> **Genetic fingerprinting** – the method of matching DNA samples found at a crime scene with a suspect

Developments in community policing

Revised

During the late twentieth century several initiatives were introduced to help improve police–community relations:

- **On the beat:** more police officers were returned to the beat to provide a visible presence on the streets.
- **Neighbourhood Watch Schemes:** first introduced in 1982, these have developed into a nationwide membership of 10 million people; they involve organised groups of local people who work with the police to prevent crime in their neighbourhood.
- **Police Community Support Officers (PCSOs):** first introduced in 2002, these help deal with anti-social behaviour and minor crime in the hope of making ordinary people feel more secure in their locality; by 2012 they numbered 16,000 (7 per cent of the force).
- **Crime Prevention Schemes:** these are run by the police and offer advice on personal safety, home and vehicle security, and protection against fraud.

Modern-day problems facing the police

Revised

- **The use of firearms by the police:** all 43 regional police forces have a number of officers trained in the use of firearms; SO19 has also been developed as the Specialist Firearms Branch.
- **Increase in police powers:** the Police and Criminal Evidence Act (1984) and the Police Act (1996) gave the police increased powers to deal with people involved in rioting, picketing and violent disorder; the Terrorism Act (2000) gave the police the right to detain a suspected terrorist for up to 48 hours and up to seven days if granted permission by a judge. These increased powers have sometimes resulted in legal challenges against police actions.
- **Pressures of red tape:** officers are required to keep written records of all dealings with the public and to record interviews held in the police station; this increase in bureaucracy has become burdensome and time-consuming for police officers.
- **Pressure from organised criminals:** developments in technology and transport have resulted in changing patterns of crime; drug trafficking is now operated by gangs on a global scale; gang culture in city areas has resulted in an increase in gun and knife crime; attacks by terrorist gangs have also been on the increase.

> **Key term**
>
> **Red tape** – time-consuming official paperwork and routines

> **Exam practice**
>
> Describe developments in policing methods during the late twentieth and twenty-first centuries. **[4 marks]**

> **Answers online**

> **Exam tip**
>
> When answering 'describe' questions you need to ensure that you include two to three key factors. To obtain maximum marks you need to support these factors with specific factual detail, in this case, describing developments in forensic science such as DNA and genetic fingerprinting, the growth of special units and developments in community policing.

Chapter 9 Changing methods of punishment in Wales and England

Key issues

You will need to demonstrate good knowledge and understanding of the key issues of this period:

- How were criminals punished, 1530–1700?
- What were the main turning points in methods of punishment, 1700–1900?
- How successful have methods of punishment been from 1900 to today?

9.1 How were criminals punished, 1530–1700?

Methods of punishment during the sixteenth and seventeenth centuries	
Continuity The primary aim of punishment was that of deterrence (making the person too frightened to commit a crime) and retribution (making the person suffer for their crime) – themes that carried on from the medieval period	**Change** The development of the idea of locking up a person in prison as a 'punishment'; the building of houses of correction and Bridewells

The use of corporal punishment

Revised ☐

The medieval system of **corporal punishment** served two purposes in the sixteenth and seventeenth centuries:

- to teach offenders how wrong they were
- to deter others from following their example (this is why the punishment took place in public).

Three main types of corporal punishment were used during this time:

- **Whipping/flogging**: flogging was used for a variety of offences such as refusing to attend church and for stealing goods worth less than a shilling (5p). The Tudor laws against vagrancy meant that beggars could be publicly disgraced by being whipped or flogged.
- **Stocks and pillory**: the main purpose of both the stocks and the pillory was to humiliate offenders in public, dissuade them from repeating their offence and serve as an example so others would not do the same. They were used to punish offenders for minor crimes such as drunkenness, swearing, and dishonest trading such as selling underweight goods. Those in the stocks or pillory could be pelted with stones and rotten food. The pillory was not finally abolished until 1837 and the stocks continued in use until 1872.

> **Key terms**
>
> **Corporal punishment** – physical punishment
>
> **Flogging** – punishment by beating
>
> **Stocks** – a wooden frame used as a public punishment with holes for the feet
>
> **Pillory** – a wooden frame used as a public punishment with holes for the head and hands

Source A: In the sixteenth century the pillory was used a form of public humiliation for minor crimes.

TWO PRETENDED FORTUNE-TELLERS IN THE PILLORY

What does Source A show you about punishment in the sixteenth century?

[2 marks]

Answers online

The use of public execution

Revised

Public execution in the sixteenth and seventeenth centuries was a continuation of the punishment administered throughout the medieval period. It was believed that public execution would deter onlookers from committing crimes themselves and would show that law and order was being maintained. There were many crimes punishable by execution, including:

- major crimes like murder, treason, counterfeiting and arson
- some minor crimes like theft of goods valued over a shilling (5p).

Examples of public execution

Revised

During the Tudor period execution was often the punishment for political and religious crimes.

- **Rowland Lee:** between 1534 and 1543 Lee, the President of the Council of Wales and the Marches, had over 5000 people publicly hanged in an effort to impose law and order.
- **The Marian Persecution:** Edward VI (1547–53) had made England completely Protestant but his successor, Mary Tudor (1553–58), turned the country back to the Roman Catholic faith and persecuted those Protestants who refused to change faith. Two hundred and eighty Protestants were publicly burnt at the stake as heretics. Mary hoped the public burning would turn people against the Protestant religion. Among the high-ranking officials burnt were Nicholas Ridley, Bishop of London; Hugh Latimer, Bishop of Gloucester; and Robert Ferrar, Bishop of St David's.

- **Mary, Queen of Scots:** Mary Tudor was succeeded by her half-sister, Elizabeth (1558–1603) who chose the Protestant faith for the kingdom. In 1586 Elizabeth's cousin, Mary, Queen of Scots, was arrested. She was accused of being at the centre of the Babington Plot, a Catholic plot which aimed to kill Elizabeth and replace her with Mary as Queen. Mary was found guilty of treason and executed in February 1587.
- **John Penry, a Welsh Puritan martyr:** as a Puritan, Penry was critical of the bishops who ran the Church of England and was involved in the publication of pamphlets which called for religious reform. In 1593 he was arrested, put on trial for treason and hanged in London.

The use of imprisonment

The idea of punishment through imprisonment had not existed during the medieval period but began to be seen as a punishment for certain types of offenders during the Tudor and Stuart period.

The introduction of houses of correction and Bridewells

Revised

During the Tudor period JPs began to set up houses of correction, sometimes known as **Bridewells**, with the aim of changing the ways of persistent beggars. In 1553 Edward VI converted the palace of Bridewell into a house of correction. It aimed to reform rather than deter by putting the inmates to supervised work. The tasks included making caps and bed covers, wool carding, silk winding and nail making. In 1576 an Act allowed for the setting up of houses of correction, based on the London Bridewell example.

The use of prison as a punishment

Revised

Before the eighteenth century prison was regarded not so much as a punishment but rather as a place to hold suspects until they were brought to trial or released. There was no set time for how long suspects could be held. The jailers received no salary and depended on forcing money from prisoners. For many prisoners, conditions were appalling and they were brutally treated.

There were fourteen prisons in London in the sixteenth century. Below are some of the most important:

Newgate	The chief criminal prison
The Clink, Southwark	For religious prisoners
Fleet, Clerkenwell	For prisoners committed by order of the monarch
Marshalsea, Southwark	For religious prisoners
The King's Bench, Southwark	For **debtors**

> **Revision tasks**
>
> Use the information in the section below to complete the following.
>
> 1. Explain why public execution was a common method of punishment during the sixteenth century.
> 2. Explain why each of the following individuals was executed: Nicholas Ridley and Hugh Latimer; Mary, Queen of Scots; John Penry.

> **Key term**
>
> **Bridewell** – a house of correction, or prison, for persistent beggars

> **Key term**
>
> **Debtor** – someone who owes money to another person

> **Revision tasks**
>
> Use the information in this section to complete the following.
>
> 1. Describe conditions inside prisons during the sixteenth and seventeenth centuries.
> 2. Explain why houses of correction were set up during the Tudor period.

9.2 What were the main turning points in methods of punishment, 1700–1900?

Methods of punishment during the eighteenth and nineteenth centuries	
Continuity To begin with, the emphasis continued to be on physical punishment and public humiliation	**Change** A change of attitude during the Victorian period towards the functions of prisons and a growing feeling that the punishment should match the crime

The development of transportation
Revised

Transportation was introduced as an alternative to the death penalty. An Act of 1678 allowed **convicts** to be sent to British colonies in North America and the West Indies.

Transportation Act (1717) – laid down a formal system with sentences of 7 years, 14 years or life

Alternative to hanging – hanging was considered too extreme for some crimes

To save money – imprisonment was expensive

To reduce crime – criminals were removed

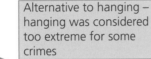
The reasons for transportation

To populate the Empire – sending convicts overseas would help colonise Britain's Empire

Reform of character – criminals could be reformed through hard work and learning new skills

To deter – hopefully the harshness of the sentence would deter others from committing such crimes

Key terms

Transportation – sending convicted criminals overseas for punishment

Convict – someone who is in prison because they are guilty of a crime

The ending of transportation to North America and the use of hulks
Revised

- Between 1717 and 1776 over 30,000 prisoners were transported to North America but the outbreak of the American War of Independence ended this trade.
- A crisis developed as Britain's prisons became overcrowded following the end of transportation.
- **Hulks** were used as emergency prison accommodation while a new outlet for transportation was sought.
- Conditions on board the overcrowded hulks were terrible; at least 25 per cent of the prisoners died from the unclean environment or the outbreaks of violence.
- Captain Cook's discovery of Australia in 1772 offered an alternative location for convicts.

Key term

Hulks – ships used as prisons

Transportation to Australia
Revised

- In May 1787, the first fleet of eleven ships carrying 736 convicts (including 200 women) set sail from Portsmouth on an eight-month voyage to Australia.
- The ships arrived at Sydney Cove (Botany Bay) in New South Wales on 26 January 1788; 40 of the 736 convicts died on the voyage.
- Between 1787 and 1867, as many as 162,000 convicts were transported to Australia – an average of 2000 convicts a year.

Punishment and conditions in Australia

Revised

- Conditions in the new penal colony were harsh for prisoners and they were flogged for even minor offences.

- Those who did not conform were sent to the harsher penal settlements like Norfolk Island, working in chain gangs at stone-breaking and building roads.

- Early release was offered as a motive for good behaviour:

○ **ticket of leave:** early release after serving four years of a seven-year sentence

○ **conditional pardon:** granted after five years of a sentence, but the person could not return to Britain

○ **certificate of freedom:** granted after full sentence had been served; the person was allowed to return to Britain.

The end of transportation

Revised

Changing attitudes to punishment, the expense of operating the system, and growing resentment from Australia at its use as a dumping ground for criminals resulted in the end of transportation:

- In 1840 transportation to New South Wales was stopped.

- In 1852 Tasmania refused to accept any more convicts.

- In 1867 Western Australia stopped taking convicts.

Revision task

Using the information in this section, explain the part played by each of the following in the history of transportation:

North America   Hulks

Australia

Exam practice

Why was transportation an important development in punishment in the eighteenth and nineteenth centuries? **[8 marks]**

Answers online

Exam tip

In the 'importance' questions you need to identify two to three key reasons why something was important, using specific factual detail to back up your comments. In this instance you should refer to how transportation offered a new approach to punishment, how it benefited Britain by getting rid of our criminals, how it colonised the Empire and served as a deterrent by making the punishment harsh.

Changes in public execution

By 1815 there were 225 **capital crimes** that were punishable by death and there was a growing feeling that there was a need to reform the **Criminal** or **Bloody Code**.

Reform of the Criminal Code (1823)

Revised

The Criminal Code, or 'Bloody' Code as it was more commonly referred to, was criticised for its harshness. Even minor crimes like stealing sheep or rabbits were punishable by death. This meant that juries were often reluctant to convict people as the punishment did not reflect the crime.

The lawyer and MP Sir Samuel Romilly campaigned for the reform of the Criminal Code and put pressure on important figures such as the Home Secretary, Sir Robert Peel. The result was a series of reforms which ended the Criminal Code:

- In 1823 Peel abolished the death penalty for half of the capital crimes.

- In 1832 the number of capital crimes was cut by a further two-thirds.

- By 1861 the number of capital crimes had been reduced to just five – murder, treason, espionage, arson in royal dockyards and piracy with violence.

The crimes punishable by public execution were now limited to just two – murder and treason.

Key terms

Capital crime – a crime punishable by the death penalty

Criminal or Bloody Code – the harsh laws gradually introduced between 1500 and 1750

Problems with public executions

Revised ☐

- Public executions like those at Tyburn, London, attracted large crowds and were viewed as entertainment.
- These large crowds were often the cause of lawlessness.
- Such executions could make heroes or martyrs out of those hanged.

- Public execution was sometimes a miscarriage of justice when an innocent person was hanged; Dic Penderyn was hanged following the Merthyr Rising in 1831 for a crime he did not commit.

The end of public execution

Revised ☐

A Royal Commission on Capital Punishment was set up in 1864 and recommended an end to public executions. Public executions were stopped in 1868. This represented a major turning point in attitudes to punishment. Between 1868 and the late 1960s, when executions ended, all hangings had to take place inside prisons.

Revision task

Copy out the table below and use the information in this section to identify three factors for each column.

Criticisms of the Criminal Code	Criticisms of public executions
1	1
2	2
3	3

The need for prison reform

The dramatic rise in the prison population following the ending of transportation to North America in 1776 caused some people to seek reform of the appalling conditions inside overcrowded prisons.

The work of the prison reformers

John Howard (1726–90)

Revised ☐

In 1776, John Howard, High Sheriff of Bedfordshire, carried out a survey of prisons. He published his findings in a book called *The State of Prisons in England and Wales* (1777). These included:

- Prisoners were often forced to stay in prison because they could not afford the discharge fee set by the jailor.
- Prisoners were not separated by the types of crime they were in prison for – debtors (who accounted for 60 per cent of the inmates) mixed with serious criminals (24 per cent of inmates).
- Many prisoners died from disease such as jail fever.

Howard believed that prisons should be used to reform criminals, clergymen should make regular visits to guide prisoners towards a better life, and prisoners should be kept in **solitary confinement**.

Key terms

Jail fever – typhus, an infectious disease common in eighteenth-century prisons

Solitary confinement – when a prisoner is kept separate from other people

Sir George Onesiphorus Paul (1746–1820)

G.O. Paul led the prison reform movement in Gloucestershire. He employed the architect William Blackburn to design a new jail for the county. Paul specified three key principles in its design:

- **Security:** it was surrounded by a 5.4 metre high wall; the building was polygonal (many-sided) to let staff see what was going on.
- **Health:** it had an isolation section to check new prisoners for disease; an exercise yard; and good ventilation.
- **Separation:** it was divided into a jail (for offenders awaiting trial) and a penitentiary (a place for punishment), as well as separate male and female areas; it also had a chapel, workrooms, and a darkened cell (for punishment).

In 1784 G.O. Paul published a book, *Thoughts on the Alarming Progress of Jail Fever*: he thought the fever could be stopped if prisons were sensibly designed.

Elizabeth Fry (1780–1845)

Fry was a devout Quaker. In 1813 she visited Newgate Prison, London and was horrified at the conditions, especially for female prisoners. She began a campaign:

- In 1817 she formed the Association for the Improvement of Women Prisoners in Newgate.
- Her campaign resulted in the appointment of female warders; the establishment of schools for women and their children; and the introduction of work (needlework) for female prisoners.
- She travelled the country and set up Ladies' Prison Committees to carry on her reforms in other prisons.

Revision task

Copy out the table and use the information in this section to complete it.

Prison reformer	Their ideas on prison reform	What was their contribution to improving conditions for prisoners?
John Howard		
G.O. Paul		
Elizabeth Fry		

The Jails Act (1823)

Revised

A major step in prison reform was the Jails Act of 1823. This ordered that JPs visit prisons on a regular basis to inspect conditions, that jailers were to be salaried, prisoners were to follow a reform programme, and that all prisoners had to be kept in secure and sanitary accommodation.

The separate and silent systems

During the Victorian period there were several experiments in prisoners' treatment:

The separate system

Revised

- Prisoners were kept in individual cells where they worked, prayed and were visited by clergymen.
- Prisoners were only allowed to leave their cells for religious services or for exercise, when they had to wear masks; this was to make them anonymous and take away their identity.
- By the 1850s over 50 prisons used the Separate System. The most famous was Pentonville Prison in London, which was built on a radial design with five wings radiating from a central point; this became the model design for all large prisons.
- Prisoners were put to work making boots, mats and prison clothes, and sewing mailbags and coal sacks.
- The separate system had a high death rate, with increased incidents of suicide and insanity.

The silent system

Revised

- As with the separate system, this method of punishment resulted in increased levels of suicide and insanity.
- This system depended on fear and hatred, with prison life being made as unpleasant as possible.
- The tasks for prisoners were designed to be as boring and pointless as possible and included the **crank**, **shot drill**, **oakum picking** and the **treadwheel**.
- The aim was to make the prisoners hate the silent system so much they would not re-offend.

Key terms

Crank – turning a crank handle a set number of times in order to earn food

Oakum picking – untwisting lengths of old tarred rope so that it could be reused

Shot drill – heavy cannonballs were passed from one to another down a long line of prisoners

Treadwheel – a revolving staircase in which prisoners walked for several hours

Later prison reform

Revised

Both the separate and silent systems failed to lower the re-offending rate. The high suicide and insanity rates led to further prison reform, which concentrated on harsh punishments:

- The 1865 Prisons Act (also known as the Penal Servitude Act) concentrated on a life of 'Hard labour, hard fare and hard board' inside prison; its aim was to impose strict punishment rather than reform.
- The 1877 Prisons Act brought all prisons under government control.

Revision tasks

Use the information in this section to complete the following.

1. Describe the key characteristics of the separate and silent systems.
2. Identify **two** differences between the systems.

Use Sources A and B and your own knowledge to explain why prisons changed in the first half of the nineteenth century. **[6 marks]**

Source A: Extract from a school textbook

'Elizabeth Fry visited Newgate Prison in London in 1813. She found men and women were mixed together. Conditions were overcrowded with 300 in one room. Some women worked as prostitutes in prison to afford food and many babies were born inside prison.'

Source B: The separate system in the 1840s

CONVICTS EXERCISING IN PENTONVILLE PRISON.

Answers online

Exam tip

In this type of question you need to identify 'change' or 'lack of change', making direct reference to the information in both sources linked to your knowledge of this topic area. In this instance you should mention that Source A notes that in 1813 men and women shared the same cells, which were overcrowded, and conditions for prisoners were terrible. This contrasts with Source B, which shows how conditions had changed by the 1840s. Prisoners were now kept in separate cells, they wore uniforms and had to hide their identity. These changes took place because of new Victorian attitudes to punishment.

9.3 How successful have methods of punishment been from 1900 to today?

Methods of punishment in the twentieth and twenty-first centuries	
Continuity Prison has continued to be seen as a place of imprisonment, a building which isolates criminals from society	**Change** A shift of attitude away from **retribution** and physical punishment towards **rehabilitation** with the ending of corporal and capital punishment and a move towards considering alternatives to prison sentences

Changing attitudes to punishment

The changing attitudes towards punishment which began in the Victorian period continued into the twentieth century.

Abolition of corporal punishment   Revised

During the twentieth century, public attitudes turned against inflicting pain as a punishment.

- In 1914 flogging male prisoners was limited as a punishment and was abolished in 1948 (it had been abolished for women in 1820).
- In 1986 it became illegal to use the cane for punishment in schools.

Key terms

Retribution – a fitting punishment for the crime committed

Rehabilitation – reforming criminals through treatment and training so they can re-enter society

Abolition of capital punishment

Revised

Attitudes towards the abolition of capital punishment strengthened during the twentieth century.

Arguments in favour of abolition	Arguments against abolition
<ul><li>An innocent person may be hanged</li><li>Hanging is not really a deterrent as most murders happen impulsively</li><li>Hanging is barbaric</li><li>Even the worst person may be reformed</li><li>The crime rate has not increased in countries which have abolished capital punishment</li><li>Hanging can make martyrs of criminals such as terrorists</li></ul>	<ul><li>Hanging is the ultimate deterrent</li><li>A dead murderer cannot kill again</li><li>Keeping a murderer in prison is expensive</li><li>A hanged murderer gets what he/she deserves</li><li>Hanging satisfies the victim's family and the public</li></ul>

Two cases in the 1950s highlighted the debate about capital punishment:

- **Derek Bentley (1933–53):** hanged after being found guilty of being an accomplice in the murder of a police officer, during a burglary. Bentley was said to have a mental age of 10 and his execution caused great controversy. The actual murderer was 16-year-old Christopher Craig, who could not be hanged because he was a juvenile.
- **Ruth Ellis (1926–55):** the last woman to be hanged in the UK after being convicted of murdering her lover David Blakely. Many claimed it was a 'crime of passion'.

These hangings strengthened the case for abolishing capital punishment.

- **The Homicide Act (1957)** abolished hanging for all murders except for the murder of a police officer, murder by shooting or murder while resisting arrest.
- **The Abolition of the Death Penalty Act (1969)** made all hanging illegal and finally ended capital punishment in the UK.
- The last hanging in the UK took place on 13 August 1964 when two men, Peter Allen and Gwynne Evans, were hanged for the murder of A.J. West, whom they had set out to rob.

Revision task

Using the information in this section, explain the part played by each of the following in the move to end capital punishment: Derek Bentley; Ruth Ellis; Homicide Act; Abolition of the Death Penalty Act.

Punishment as retribution or rehabilitation

Revised

The twentieth century witnessed a long debate between the contrasting views of punishment:

- **Retribution:** imprisonment itself was not 'the punishment'; prisoners should undertake hard labour, be locked up in solitary cells and not have visitors; a view inherited from the Victorian period.

- **Rehabilitation:** prison was 'the punishment'; being locked up and losing freedom was punishment in itself; prisoners should be helped to change their attitudes and behaviour through counselling, education and training; a view dominant in the second half of the twentieth century.

Changes to imprisonment

The abolition of corporal and capital punishment meant that, during the twentieth century, there were changes to imprisonment.

The use of borstals

Revised

An Act of 1908 set up the system of using **borstals** for the punishment of 15- to 21-year-olds. Borstals were organised along very strict rules and were designed to be educational rather than places of punishment. The use of corporal punishment (the **birch**) was abolished in 1962. In 1969 the minimum age to be sent to borstal was raised to 17 years. Borstals were finally abolished in 1982.

Key terms

Borstal – a place of imprisonment for reforming young offenders

Birch – a type of cane used for punishment

Young Offenders' Institutions

Revised

Violent young offenders were placed into Youth Custody. This removed them from their bad environment and attempted to reform them. In 1988 Detention Centres were replaced by Young Offenders' Institutions, which are again meant for reform. They cater for 18- to 21-year-olds and inmates receive 25 hours of education a week.

Apart from the Young Offenders' Institutions, offenders under the age of 21 can be given a custodial sentence at these other places:

- **Secure Training Centres:** these house vulnerable young people up to the age of 17 in a secure environment and aim to prevent re-offending through education and rehabilitation.
- **Local Authority Secure Children's Homes:** these focus on the physical, emotional and behavioural needs of vulnerable young people.
- **Juvenile Prisons:** these are for 15- to 18-year-old offenders and focus on reform.

Open prisons

Revised

Open prisons became popular after the Second World War as a way of relieving pressure on overcrowded prisons. They house non-violent prisoners with a low risk of escaping. Their aim is to resettle prisoners into the community. Open prisons have been criticised as being a 'soft option' though they are cheaper to run than closed prisons.

Revision tasks

Copy out the table and use the information in this section to complete it.

Institution	Type of offender sent to this institution	Description of treatment given to prisoners at this institution
Borstal		
Young Offenders' Institution		
Local Authority Secure Children's Home		
Open prison		

Prisons today

Revised

The prison population in England and Wales has continued to rise – up from 48,000 prisoners in 1985 to 88,000 in 2011. Prisoners are divided into four categories based on the type of crime they committed, their sentence and the danger they pose to the public if they escaped. Category A prisoners are those whose escape would be highly dangerous to the public, while Category D prisoners can be trusted not to try to escape and are given the privileges of an open prison. There are separate prisons for women prisoners. The largest is Holloway Prison in London.

Alternatives to imprisonment

Several factors – such as the expense of running prisons, the pressure of overcrowding and the record number of offenders – have resulted in alternative punishments which avoid lengthy prison sentences.

Suspended sentence
- Introduced in 1967
- The offender does not go to prison unless he/she commits another offence during the period of suspension.

Probation
- Introduced in 1907
- The offender follows a set of rules, keeps in touch with a probation officer and reports weekly to the police.
- Since 1982 offenders on probation have to do activities and attend day centres for up to 60 days.

Alternative punishments

Electronic tagging
- Introduced in the 1990s
- Offenders wear an electronic tag which allows the police (through GPS, global positioning satellite) to keep a watch on the offender's exact movements.
- Offenders cannot break their curfew.

Community service
- Introduced in 1972
- Offenders have to work, unpaid, for a set number of hours in the community.
- 'Community Payback' was introduced in 2003 with the aim of forcing offenders to repay the community for the wrong they have done, e.g. graffiti removal, gardening and repair projects.

Parole
- Introduced in 1967
- Offenders can be released before the end of their sentence as a reward for good behaviour and for promising to follow a set of rules.

Revision task

Use the information in this section to complete the following:
1. Explain the meaning and purpose of each of the following types of punishment:
> Suspended sentence
> Community service
> Electronic tagging
2. Using your knowledge, for each of these punishments give one advantage and one disadvantage of using it.

Exam practice

How far have attitudes towards the treatment of offenders changed from Tudor times to the present day?

[10 marks + 3 marks for SPaG]

Answers online

Exam tip

In this type of 'synoptic' essay you need to examine how attitudes have changed over a period of time – in this instance attitudes towards punishment from the 1530s to the present day – making sure you cover the whole period. You should start with the Tudor and Stuart period, then show any continuity/change into the Victorian period. You can then mention the separate and silent systems, and how rehabilitation was introduced in the twentieth century. You must ensure you cover at least three time frames.

Chapter 10 Developments in medical knowledge

Key issues

You will need to demonstrate good knowledge and understanding of the key issues of this period:

- What were the main medical ideas common in the late Middle Ages?
- What were the main developments in medical knowledge, 1500–1700?
- How much progress has been made in medical knowledge from the nineteenth century to today?

10.1 What were the main medical ideas common in the late Middle Ages?

The idea of alchemy

Revised ☐

What was alchemy?

- **Alchemy** originated in the ancient civilisations of China, India and Greece.
- It came to Europe in the late Middle Ages when ancient writings were translated into Latin, the common language at that time.
- It was a mixture of science, philosophy and **mysticism**.
- During the Middle Ages alchemists attempted to find the means to use alchemy to make:
  - ○ ordinary base metal turn into gold
  - ○ an '**elixir** of life' to make a person immortal or forever youthful.
- One of the first Englishmen to be interested in alchemy was Francis Bacon (1214–92).

Key terms

Alchemy – a type of chemistry in the Middle Ages that aimed to find a way to change ordinary metals into gold and a medicine to cure any disease

Mysticism – the belief that there is a hidden meaning to life

Elixir – a liquid with magical power that would prolong life indefinitely

The search for drugs and potions

Medieval alchemists believed that all matter was composed of four elements – air, fire, earth and water – and each had different qualities that could be observed in nature during the different seasons:

- Air was hot and moist in spring.
- Fire was hot and dry in summer.
- Earth was cold and dry in autumn.
- Water was cold and moist in winter.

Through their experiments in search of the 'elixir of life', medieval alchemists developed new equipment and technology for extracting chemicals, refining liquids and mixing potions. Thus they:

- produced hydrochloric acid, nitric acid, potash and sodium carbonate
- identified the elements arsenic, antimony and bismuth.

By these means they laid the foundation for the development of chemistry as a scientific discipline.

Revision task

Write a brief explanation of each of the following terms:
- Alchemist
- The four elements
- The elixir of life

In the Middle Ages doctors were called physicians. They trained at a university medical school and used a variety of methods when treating a patient, including the urine chart and the 'zodiac man' chart:

The urine chart

- This was a basic tool that doctors used to diagnose illnesses.
- Urine samples were matched against a colour on a urine chart and a written description for that colour; this helped the physician to make a diagnosis.

The 'zodiac man' chart and the influence of astrology

- Medieval physicians used **astrology** to help treat patients.
- They believed the movement of the planets affected people's health.
- They needed to know the position of the planets when diagnosing illnesses and deciding on a treatment.
- They consulted a book called the *Valemecum*, which contained the signs of the zodiac and 'zodiac man' charts.
- By consulting the chart and the position of the stars, they could work out which treatments could be used on certain parts of the body at that time.
- Each sign of the zodiac was associated with different parts of the body. Physicians would avoid operating on that part of the body when its star sign was in the sky, e.g. the Aries ram was linked to the head and so they avoided treating head-related problems when Aries was in the sky.

> **Key term**
>
> **Astrology** – the study of the planets and how they might influence people's lives

The Theory of the Four Humours

- This theory was developed by ancient Greek and Roman doctors, and continued to dominate medicine in the Middle Ages.
- It was believed that the body contained four important liquids called **humours**.
- If the humours stayed in balance then a person remained healthy.
- A person became ill when the humours became unbalanced, or when there was too much of one humour and not enough of another.
- The body got rid of excess humours through sweat, urine and faeces; when this did not happen enough, illness occurred and treatment was needed.
- The treatment involved getting the humours within the body back into balance and this might require removing excess liquid:
  - Excess blood was removed by making the patient bleed.
  - Excess bile was removed by making the patient vomit.

> **Key term**
>
> **Humours** – four liquids (phlegm, blood, black bile and yellow bile) in the body, that were related to the four seasons and to the four elements (air, fire, earth and water), and believed to cause illness when they became unbalanced

Blood
- Spring – caused blood to increase, especially among children, and led to dysentery and nose bleeds.
- Air – hot and moist

Yellow bile
Summer – yellow bile would increase, especially among young people, and led to fevers and vomiting.
Fire – hot and dry

The Theory of the Four Humours
(and their links to the four seasons and the four elements)

Black bile
Autumn – fevers would lessen but black bile would increase, especially among adults.
Earth – cold and dry

Phlegm
- Winter – phlegm increased in winter, especially among the old, because the weather was chilly and wet.
- Water – cold and moist

Key terms

Bile – either of two bodily humours, one of which (black bile) was thought to cause depression and the other (yellow bile) anger

Phlegm – one of the four humours; a thick substance produced in the nose and throat

Continuity of ideas

Revised

In the Middle Ages the medical ideas put forward by doctors in ancient Greece and Rome were still followed. Two of the most important of these ancient doctors were Hippocrates and Galen.

- **Hippocrates** – a Greek doctor from 400BC who wrote medical books; he developed the idea of clinical observation (observing and recording the symptoms and development of an illness or disease); he also developed the theory of the four humours to explain the causes of disease and help with treatment; he has been called the 'father of modern medicine'.

- **Galen** – born in Greece, he lived between AD129 and 203; he gained his knowledge of **anatomy** from treating injured gladiators in Rome; he wrote medical books, and gave lectures and anatomical demonstrations; he revived the ideas of Hippocrates, especially the importance of observation and recording; he believed in the four humours and encouraged **blood-letting** as a treatment for disease.

Key terms

Anatomy – the study of how the human skeleton fits together

Blood-letting – the removal of blood through deliberate bleeding

Had medical knowledge advanced by the end of the Middle Ages?

Revised

- There was little advancement – doctors continued to follow the ideas of the ancient writers and believed in the Theory of the Four Humours.

- Some doctors, however, did come to believe that God and the Devil influenced health; epidemics like the **Black Death** were seen as punishments from God for leading a sinful life.

- It was not until the time of the **Renaissance** in the sixteenth century that any real advances in medical knowledge were made.

Key terms

Black Death – a form of bubonic plague that spread across Europe during the mid-fourteenth century, killing 50 million people

Renaissance – rebirth of culture and learning, especially in art, literature and music; it marked the transition from the medieval to the modern period

What does Source A show you about medical ideas in the late Middle Ages? **[2 marks]**

Source A: A 'zodiac man' chart from a medieval doctor's handbook. The star signs advised when not to operate on a particular part of the human body.

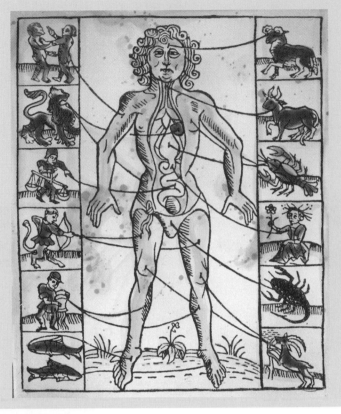

Copy out the table below and use the information in this section to complete it.

	How physicians used this method to treat patients
Urine chart	
Zodiac chart	
Theory of Four Humours	
Work of Hippocrates	
Work of Galen	

In this type of question, you need to pick out specific details from what you can see in the source and its caption. In this instance you need to say that doctors in the Middle Ages used astrology to help treat patients; they believed the planets affected people's health and they had to consult the zodiac chart and the position of the stars before they decided on what treatment to give.

10.2 What were the main developments in medical knowledge, 1500–1700?

The impact of the Renaissance

Revised

During the sixteenth century there was a rebirth or 'Renaissance' in learning and science, especially in the study of the achievements of the ancient Greeks and Romans. The Renaissance started in Italy before 1500 and spread across Europe. Progress in medical knowledge made great advances during the Renaissance period.

Developments in the printing press

The spread of the ideas of the Renaissance was made easier through the invention of the mechanical printing press by Johannes Gutenberg in Germany, c.1440. The printing press was first used in Britain by William Caxton in 1476. Medical books written by the ancient Greeks, Romans and the Arabs could now be printed, allowing the spread of medical knowledge and herbal remedies.

Voyages of discovery

During the late fifteenth and early sixteenth centuries, Spanish and Portuguese sailors began to make voyages of exploration:

- In 1492 Christopher Columbus discovered the 'New World' of the Americas and brought back new herbs, plants and medicines to Europe.
- The explorers Bartholomew Diaz and Vasco da Gama explored the Indian Ocean, bringing back spices and medicinal plants to Europe.
- Among the newly discovered medicinal plants were:
  - **sassafras:** the dried bark of roots, this was used as a stimulant
  - **coca:** the dried leaves provided the source for cocaine
  - **cinchona:** the bark of this tree was used to treat fevers, including malaria; it came to be known as quinine in Europe
  - **tobacco:** these dried leaves were thought to be a wonder drug!

- The discovery of these new plants helped the development of medical knowledge in Europe.

Renaissance art

The Renaissance produced many skilful artists and scholars who helped the advancement of medical knowledge:

- **Michelangelo:** he studied the muscles and limbs of the human body; he produced sculptures like the statue of 'David' and painted the human body in great detail.
- **Leonardo da Vinci:** through practical **dissection** he was able to produce detailed drawings of the human skeleton, its muscles and organs; his illustrations were printed in books, which helped further medical understanding.

New technology

The Renaissance resulted in the invention of new scientific machines such as the thermometer and microscope, both of which helped improve medical observation. (See Chapter 11.1 for more on the invention of the microscope.)

> **Revision task**
>
> Explain how each of the following factors helped the advancement of medical knowledge:
>
> - The printing press • Voyages of discovery • The Renaissance

> **Key term**
>
> **Dissection** – cutting open and examining the structure of a dead body

Important developments in medical knowledge

Several Renaissance thinkers made important contributions to the advancement of medical knowledge in specific fields of enquiry.

Observation and experience: Theophrastus Paracelsus (1493–1541)

Revised

- In 1523 Paracelsus became a medical lecturer in Basel University, Switzerland.
- He rejected the ideas of Galen, believing that disease attacked the body from outside and people needed to take medical remedies to help fight the illness.
- He insisted on observation and experience, which resulted in a more scientific approach to investigating illnesses.
- Some doctors rejected the ideas of Paracelsus because these challenged long-held views.

Study of anatomy: Andreas Vesalius (1514–64)

Revised

- At the age of just 23, Vesalius became Professor of Anatomy at Padua University in Italy.
- He worked alongside Renaissance artists dissecting corpses in order to better understand the human anatomy (see page 108).
- In 1543 he published his famous book *The Fabric of the Human Body*, which contained fine anatomical drawings.
- He questioned the views of Galen and, through dissection, proved that Galen had been wrong in some of his observations.
- Opposition from older doctors caused Vesalius to move from Padua University to become physician to Emperor Charles V and King Philip II of Spain.

Vesalius was a significant figure:

- Before Vesalius, doctors believed the books of Galen and other ancient writers were completely accurate and contained all the knowledge a doctor needed to know.
- Vesalius showed that Galen was wrong in some important details of human anatomy.
- His insistence on dissection of human, not animal, bodies introduced new scientific methods of enquiry and helped further medical knowledge.

Improved surgery: Ambroise Paré (c.1510–90)

Revised

- Born in Laval, France, Paré served as an apprentice barber surgeon (see page 116).
- In 1536 he became an army surgeon and spent twenty years treating wounded soldiers.
- The traditional method of treating battlefield wounds was to **cauterise** them with boiling oil, which was painful for the patient and caused infection; following an amputation, the bleeding was stopped by sealing the arteries with a red-hot iron.
- Paré experimented with alternative methods; he discovered that wounds healed more quickly if covered with bandages rather than using boiling oil; he also stopped cauterising wounds and instead tied the ends of arteries using silk thread called **ligatures**.
- In 1562 Paré published his *Five Books of Surgery*. He followed this in 1575 with *The Collected Works of Surgery*, which provided the latest research on amputations, setting fractures, and the treatment of wounds.
- Paré is often referred to as the 'father of modern surgery'.

> ### Key terms
>
> **Cauterise** – a method of treating amputated limbs or wounds by burning them with hot iron or oil to prevent infection, stop the bleeding and seal the wound
>
> **Ligature** – a thread tied around a vessel to constrict the flow of blood

Knowledge of the heart: William Harvey (1578–1657)

Revised

- Born in Folkestone, Kent, Harvey studied medicine in Cambridge and Padua Universities before becoming a doctor and then a lecturer in anatomy.
- Harvey believed in the importance of observation and experimentation to increase his knowledge.
- Before Harvey, most doctors believed in Galen's idea that new blood was constantly manufactured in the liver to replace blood that was burned up in the body.
- Through dissecting live animals to study the movement of the muscles in the heart, Harvey proved that blood flowed around the body and it was carried away from the heart in arteries and returned to the heart in veins; he proved that the heart acted as a pump.
- In 1628 he published his findings in his book, *An Anatomical Account of the Motion of the Heart and Blood in Animals*.

Importance of Vesalius, Paré and Harvey

Revised

Vesalius, Paré and Harvey adopted a scientific approach to the study of medicine; they believed in the importance of observation and experimentation; they helped the advancement of medical knowledge through publishing their research.

> ### Revision task
>
> Copy out the table below and use the information in this section to complete it.
>
> | | How this person contributed to the advancement of medical knowledge |
> |---|---|
> | Paracelsus | |
> | Vesalius | |
> | Paré | |
> | Harvey | |

10.3 How much progress has been made in medical knowledge from the nineteenth century to today?

Work on germ theory

- In the early nineteenth century the medieval belief still existed that **miasma** (bad air) was the cause of disease. Known as the theory of **spontaneous generation**, this was the belief that poisonous fumes given off by decaying material were blown around, causing disease to spread.
- Improvements in microscopes in the late seventeenth century led to the discovery of micro-organisms, but their link to the spread of disease was not made.
- The scientists who made the link that germs caused disease were the French chemist Louis Pasteur and the German pathologist Robert Koch.
- Their scientific investigations gave rise to '**germ theory**', the belief that some **micro-organisms** or **microbes** called bacteria caused disease.

> ### Key terms
>
> **Miasma** – smells or emissions from decomposing material that were believed to cause disease
>
> **Spontaneous generation** – the belief that living organisms could develop rapidly from decaying material
>
> **Germ theory** – the theory that all infectious diseases are caused by micro-organisms
>
> **Micro-organisms (or microbes)** – tiny single-celled living organisms too small to be seen by the naked eye, such as disease-causing bacteria

The work of Louis Pasteur (1822–95)

Revised

Pasteur carried out scientific research at several French universities before being appointed Professor of Chemistry at the Sorbonne University in Paris in 1867. His most important research included the following:

- **Pasteurisation:** one of Pasteur's first successes was helping brewers find out why barrels of alcohol were going bad. Using his microscope, he discovered that micro-organisms (specifically, germs) were growing in the brewing liquid. He found that boiling the liquid killed the harmful germs. This process came to be called **pasteurisation**. It was soon used to stop milk turning sour, as well as beer, wine and vinegar going bad.

> ### Key term
>
> **Pasteurisation** – the process of heating liquids to destroy harmful micro-organisms

- **Germ theory:** In 1860, the French Academy of Science organised a competition to prove, or disprove, the theory of 'spontaneous generation'. Pasteur believed that microbes in the air caused decay so he carried out some experiments. He filled a swan-necked (curved) flask with broth, boiled it to create sterile air and then did the same with an ordinary flask, which was left open to the air. He proved there was no decay in the sterile flask but microbes grew in the other flask. He also found that heating these microbes killed them. In 1861 Pasteur published his 'germ theory'.

↑ **Pasteur's test of spontaneous generation**

Broth is boiled — Broth remains free of micro-organisms — Curved neck is removed — Micro-organisms grow in broth

- **The silkworm disease:** in 1865 Pasteur began to study **pébrine**. He was able to prove that a particular micro-organism was responsible for the disease. He had proved the link between germs and disease.

- **Chicken cholera vaccine:** in 1879 Pasteur began to research **chicken cholera**. He extracted the germ that caused chicken cholera disease and began to inject chickens with different strengths of the disease. He found that leaving the germ exposed to air weakened it, and if this weakened germ was then injected into the chickens it prevented them from catching chicken cholera. Pasteur had discovered a vaccine (see page 118) for this disease.

- **The anthrax vaccine:** in 1876, Robert Koch (see below) successfully isolated the germ that caused **anthrax**. Pasteur's team developed a weak solution of the anthrax germ and in 1881 they began experiments vaccinating sheep. When subjected to the disease, the inoculated sheep were unaffected while those not vaccinated died from the illness. Pasteur had discovered a vaccine for anthrax.

- **The rabies vaccine:** in 1882 Pasteur began to investigate **rabies** and by 1885 he had successfully developed a vaccine.

> **Key terms**
>
> **Pébrine** – a disease of silkworms
>
> **Chicken cholera** – an acute infection of the bowels seen in chickens
>
> **Anthrax** – a highly infectious and often fatal disease affecting cattle and sheep
>
> **Rabies** – an acute infectious disease of the nervous system spread by the saliva of infected dogs

The work of Robert Koch (1843–1910)

Revised

- Koch was a German doctor who played a major role in furthering the work of Pasteur. The latter had shown the connection between germs, decay and disease; Koch took this a stage further and linked a particular germ or microbe to a particular disease.

- In 1872 Koch began a study of anthrax; by 1875, by studying the blood of affected and unaffected animals, he had identified the bacterium that caused anthrax.

- In 1878 he began research into the bacterium that caused septicaemia (blood poisoning); as the microbe was impossible to see he used a purple dye to stain it, enabling it to be seen under a microscope; he devised a way to grow the germs; he connected a new kind of lens to his microscope and photographed the germs.

- Koch also developed a solid **culture** on which to breed colonies of germs.

- Through further experiments, he isolated other germs – the **tuberculosis** or TB germ (1882) and the cholera germ (1883).

> **Key terms**
>
> **Culture** – the experimental growth of micro-organisms in a jelly-like substance
>
> **Tuberculosis** – often abbreviated to TB, it is a serious infectious disease that affects the lungs

The search for cures – developing the work of Pasteur and Koch

- **The cure for diphtheria:** Emil Behring found that animals produced anti-toxins to fight harmful bacteria; he took blood from animals that had recovered from **diphtheria** and injected it into a human patient with diphtheria; the patient recovered.

- **The syphilis germ and Salvarsan 606:** Paul Ehrlich continued Koch's experiments of injecting dyes into the bloodstream; he discovered that **antibodies** killed particular germs; he called them 'magic bullets'; he and his research team developed a new drug (Salvarsan 606) which, when injected into the bloodstream, killed the **syphilis** germ.

Key terms

Diphtheria – a serious infectious disease that causes fever and difficulty in breathing and swallowing

Antibody – a substance made in a person's blood which fights infection

Syphilis – a sexually transmitted disease

The achievements of Pasteur and Koch

Pasteur	Koch

- He developed 'germ theory' – that germs were the cause of disease.
- He discovered that heating liquids kills germs – a process called 'pasteurisation'.
- He developed vaccines for
  ○ chicken cholera (1880)
  ○ anthrax (1881)
  ○ rabies (1885).
- He used Edward Jenner's (see page 118) practice of vaccination to stop anthrax after isolating the germ that caused the disease.
	- He was a pioneer of the new science of 'bacteriology', proving that a specific germ caused a particular disease.
	- He identified the germ that caused tuberculosis (TB) in 1882 and cholera in 1883.
	- His work caused the German government to set up the Institute of Infectious Diseases in Berlin in 1891.
	- In 1905 he was awarded the Nobel Prize for his research.

Exam practice

How important was the work of Louis Pasteur and Robert Koch in the development of medical knowledge in the nineteenth century? **[8 marks]**

Answers online

Exam tip

In the 'how important' questions you need to identify two to three key reasons why something was important and use specific detail to back up your comments. In this instance you should comment that Pasteur's discovery of the germ theory was important because it led to the discovery of the causes of many different diseases like typhus and rabies. You should then note that Pasteur also developed methods of vaccination and immunisation against some diseases; that Koch developed this work further by isolating the bacteria responsible for TB, cholera and anthrax; and that both men played very important roles in the development of medical knowledge.

Revision task

Test your understanding of this section by writing out brief explanations of each of the following terms:

- Germ theory
- Pasteurisation
- Vaccine
- Bacteriology

The development of scanning techniques

The work of Wilhelm Röntgen (1845–1923)

Revised

- In 1895 Wilhelm Röntgen, Professor of Physics at the University of Würzburg in Germany, discovered **X-rays**.
- He was experimenting with electro-magnetic cathode rays when he discovered that they would pass through items like paper, wood, rubber and human flesh but not through bone or metal.
- The first ever X-ray photograph was of the hand of Röntgen's wife, which was published in December 1895.
- Significance: X-rays enabled surgeons to look inside the patient without surgery and marked the beginning of non-invasive surgery.
- X-rays really became important during the First World War, enabling doctors to locate deeply lodged bullets and shrapnel inside the bodies of soldiers.

> **Key term**
>
> **X-ray** – a picture produced by exposing photographic film to X-radiation (made up of X-rays), a form of electro-magnetic radiation; doctors use these images to see the bone structure of parts of the body

Modern scanning techniques

Revised

The second half of the twentieth century saw the development of a new range of scanning techniques, which transformed doctors' abilities to see inside the body without invasive surgery.

Ultrasound scanning

This has developed since the 1950s. Unlike X-rays, which use radiation, ultrasound scanning uses high-frequency sound waves to produce 3D images of the inside of the body. It is used to see pictures of a foetus inside the womb and to examine the body's internal organs.

MRI scan

First used in 1977, the magnetic resonance imaging (MRI) scanner uses a strong magnetic field and radio waves to create pictures of tissues, organs and features inside the body on a computer. Short bursts of radio waves are sent through the body by the scanner; the signals sent back are different for hard and soft tissue, enabling a detailed picture of the internal body to be made.

MRI scans are used to take pictures of the brain and spinal cord to detect abnormalities and tumours.

PET scanning

Positron emission tomography (PET) scanning has been in use since the early 1970s and involves the injection of a radioactive trace chemical into a vein of the patient's body. The scanner detects the movement of the trace chemical through the body, enabling a 3D image of the body to be generated. PET scanning differs from other scans in revealing details of cells or an organ or tissue. It is used to detect cancer, brain diseases and heart problems.

CT scanning

Computerised tomography (CT) scanning was first introduced in the 1970s. This machine sends several X-rays through the body at the same time from different angles, building up a 2D image on the computer monitor. It produces a more detailed picture than X-rays. It is used to pinpoint tumours and to direct radiotherapy to certain body areas.

Revision task

Copy out the table and complete it using the information in this section.

Scanning technique	How it works	What it is used for
Ultrasound		
MRI		
PET		
CT		

Developments in genetics

Genes are the means through which living organisms inherit features from their ancestors. Children look like their parents because they inherit their parents' genes. The study of this process is **genetics**.

Key terms

Gene – part of the nucleus of a cell that determines how our bodies look and work

Genetics – the study of what genes are, how they work and how they are passed on

The discovery of DNA

Revised

In the early twentieth century, scientists knew **DNA** existed and that it carried genetic information, but they did not know how it did this. It took a series of discoveries over a long period to unravel its secrets

- Rosalind Franklin, a British biophysicist and chemist, developed a technique called X-ray diffraction to photograph a single strand of DNA; the physicist and molecular biologist Maurice Wilkins worked with her and passed on the first photographs of DNA structure to two Cambridge scientists, Francis Crick and James Watson.

- Crick and Watson discovered that the structure of DNA was a double helix, or a pair of interlocking spirals joined by bases like rungs on a ladder; they also proved that this DNA blueprint was passed on from one generation to the next.

- Their discovery has been regarded as one of the major medical triumphs of the twentieth century; in 1962 Watson, Crick and Wilkins were awarded the Nobel Prize for medicine (Franklin had died in 1958).

Key term

DNA – Deoxyribonucleic Acid, the molecule that genes are made of

Mapping the human genome

Revised

- In 1990 the Human **Genome** Project was set up to identify the role of each of the 100,000 genes in a human DNA molecule and to compile a complete map of human DNA.

- Research teams from eighteen countries took part and it was completed in 2003.

- This was an important development in medical knowledge – it provided the complete genetic blueprint of a human being.

Key term

Genome – complete set of chromosomes and genes that an individual organism inherits

Continued development and application

Revised

- **Genetic engineering:** as a result of the work on DNA, scientists identified that the causes of some illnesses are genetic; scientists have used genetic engineering to create new varieties of plants and animals, through genetic modification or cloning (e.g. Dolly the sheep).

- **Genetic screening and testing:** this has been used for preventative medicine; patients most likely to get diseases like cancer are screened and this helps them avoid activities that might trigger the cancer to start.

- **Gene therapy:** this involves the theory of using genes from healthy people to cure the sick; developments in this area are still in their early stages.

Revision task

Construct your own mind map or spider diagram to show the key developments in genetics during the twentieth and twenty-first centuries.

Chapter 11 Changes in the prevention and treatment of disease

Key issues

You will need to demonstrate good knowledge and understanding of the key issues of this period:

- How did methods of treating disease change from the late Middle Ages to the eighteenth century?
- What were the main advances made in surgical methods in Britain in the nineteenth century?
- What have been the main turning points from the twentieth century to today?

11.1 How did methods of treating disease change from the late Middle Ages to the eighteenth century?

The use of traditional treatments and remedies

The use of herbal medicines
Revised

Throughout the Middle Ages, most illnesses were treated with herbal potions:

- Doctors and women healers possessed a large store of knowledge about using herbs to treat everyday illnesses.
- Many locally-grown plants were used but exploration during the sixteenth century allowed the use of foreign plants such as sugar, which became a common ingredient after 1492.
- The herbs were ground with a **pestle and mortar**; liquid was added to make a herbal drink, or the herbs were mixed with plant oil to make an ointment.
- Books like the *Leech Book* of Bald, an Anglo-Saxon physician in the tenth century, provided many remedies which actually worked.
- The herb plantain was a common ingredient in the *Leech Book*, being recommended for boils in the ear, dog bites, and other cuts and wounds.
- In thirteenth century in Wales a family of doctors – Rhiwallon Feddyg and his sons Cadwgan, Gruffudd and Einion – served as physicians to the Lords of Dinefwr in Carmarthenshire; they became known as the 'Doctors of Myddfai' and they recorded their medical cures and remedies in a manuscript which is now known as *The Red Book of Hergest*.
- The invention of the printing press made it possible for books called **herbals** to be produced; clergyman and physician William Turner (c.1510–68) was the author of two important works:
  - *Names of Herbs* (1548)
  - *A New Herbal* (1551).

Key terms

Pestle and mortar – a club-shaped tool (pestle) used for mixing or grinding substances in a bowl (mortar)

Herbals – books describing and listing the medical properties of plants

- Upper-class women were expected to acquire medical knowledge as part of their education and were known as 'housewife physicians'; they treated their families and servants and people from their village and local farms.
  - Lady Grace Mildmay (1552–1620) provided medical care and wrote books containing recipes for fevers, coughs, stomach pains and smallpox.
  - Lady Fettiplace's *Receipt Book* (1604) and *The Accomplish't Lady's Delight* (1675) contained remedies for treating illnesses.

Barber surgeons

Revised

- **Barber surgeons** were the most common medical practitioners during the Middle Ages, performing tasks such as blood-letting, extracting teeth, performing minor surgery, selling medicines and cutting hair.
- They learnt their trade by being apprenticed to a more experienced colleague.
- Surgery was not taught in most medical schools, and barber surgeons were looked down on by physicians, who had been trained at medical school.
- They carried on their trade in a shop open to the street, advertising their services by a red and white pole (white stood for bandages, red for blood).

- As tradesmen, barber surgeons were granted a Royal Charter in 1540 by King Henry VIII, becoming the 'Company of Barber Surgeons'.
- In 1745 surgeons split from barbers – surgery was then recognised as a profession while barber surgeons continued to offer their trade to the less well off.
- They were limited in what they could do; due to the pain factor and the danger from blood loss, they had to work quickly.
- The treatment used most, apart from blood-letting, was cautery – using a hot iron to burn away diseased tissue, seal wounds and stop bleeding.

Blood-letting, leeches and purging

Revised

The Theory of the Four Humours continued to be followed beyond the Middle Ages. It was believed that imbalances in the human body, which caused illnesses, could only be restored through blood-letting or purging.

- Blood-letting was the most common way of treating illness. This was done either by making an incision in a person's vein and draining the blood (a process called 'venesection') or by putting leeches on a person's body and allowing them to suck out the blood.
  - Incisions were used when large amounts of blood needed to be drained. Moderate amounts of blood were obtained by using a bleeding cup, which was heated and placed over a tiny cut to draw out blood by suction.
  - Small amounts were obtained by using blood-sucking leeches.
  - There is little evidence to suggest that blood-letting was of any use in treating most diseases.
- Purging involved pumping a liquid into the bowels through the rectum, using a tube and a pig's bladder to act as a pump; the liquid purge was made up of herbs, honey and water.

Scientific approaches to treating disease

During the eighteenth century, modern science began to develop through detailed observation, experimentation and measurement. The beliefs of the ancient writers of medicine began to be challenged through these processes and the invention of new technology.

The invention of the microscope

Revised

The Renaissance stimulated the development of new inventions such as the microscope, which helped the advancement of medical knowledge:

- In 1590 the Dutch spectacle (glasses) maker Hans Jansen used two lenses to make a simple microscope (the compound microscope).
- In 1609 Galileo Galilei developed a compound microscope with a convex and a concave lens.
- During the 1660s and 1670s Marcello Malpighi, an Italian doctor, used the microscope to study blood; he discovered minute blood vessels (capillaries) that link arteries and veins.

- In 1665 Robert Hooke, an Englishman, further developed the microscope and published his *Micrographia*, which contained detailed engravings of tiny organisms, such as the flea and louse, as seen under the microscope.
- In 1674 Anthony van Leeuwenhoek, a Dutch clockmaker, made improvements to the lens of the microscope, which enabled him to see tiny objects, such as fleas, more clearly.
- By 1830 developments in the production of purer glass enabled Joseph Lister, a British scientist, to develop a stronger microscope (which magnified one thousand times without distortion), which enabled the study of micro-organisms in greater detail.

Scientific study of disease

Revised

By the eighteenth century, a more scientific approach to the study of disease was being followed. As part of their training, doctors had to carry out dissections, use microscopes and think scientifically. As a result, the ideas in the medical books of the ancient writers were questioned:

- It was discovered that the theory of the four elements, which formed the basis of the Theory of the Four Humours, was wrong.
- It was discovered that the air was made up of different gasses – Robert Boyle carried out experiments on air, **combustion** and **respiration**, which resulted in Boyle's Law (1665).
- New medicines were discovered through scientific study – during the 1780s, William Withering analysed the ingredients in the herbal remedy for **dropsy**; through experiments he discovered that the foxglove plant (*Digitalis purpura*) was used as a drug to treat heart disease; in 1785 he published *An Account of the Foxglove and some of its Medical Uses*.

Key terms

Combustion – the process of burning

Respiration – the process of breathing

Dropsy – a disease which causes the accumulation of fluid in the human body

Edward Jenner and vaccination

Revised

Since the sixteenth century, outbreaks of smallpox had regularly swept across Europe. It was spread by coughing, sneezing and personal contact with an infected person. The disease had a high death rate and there was no cure. Those who survived were often left deaf, blind, brain damaged, physically disabled and disfigured by pock marks. During the eighteenth century two methods of preventing smallpox were developed – **inoculation** and **vaccination**.

Inoculation

- Inoculation first developed in China and from there spread through Asia to Turkey. It involved spreading matter from a smallpox scab onto an open cut on a healthy person's skin, giving them a mild dose of the disease and so protecting them from the full effects of smallpox.

Key terms

Inoculation – to put a low dose of a disease into the body to help it fight against a more serious attack of the disease

Vaccination – injecting a harmless form of a disease into a person or animal to prevent them from getting that disease

- Lady Mary Wortley Montagu, whilst living in Constantinople (Istanbul), had her young son inoculated in 1718. When she returned to London in 1721 she had her daughter inoculated. She persuaded others to do the same.
- Inoculation became popular but it was not completely safe. Some patients died because they contracted a fatal form of the disease.

Vaccination

A safer method of preventing the smallpox disease was developed by Edward Jenner (1749–1823).

- Edward Jenner was a country doctor. He experimented to try to find out why milkmaids who had suffered from cowpox never caught smallpox.
- In 1796 he injected a small boy, James Phipps, with the pus from the sores of a milkmaid with cowpox; Phipps developed cowpox; when he recovered he was given a dose of smallpox; Phipps did not develop smallpox.
- Jenner had found a way of making people immune from a deadly infectious disease without the risks of inoculation; he called this method vaccination (after the Latin word *vacca*, meaning cow).
- Jenner published his findings in a book *An Inquiry into the Causes and Effects of the Variolae Vaccinae* (1798); at first there was considerable opposition to his ideas.
- In 1802 the government awarded him a grant of £30,000 to open a vaccination clinic in London; in 1852 the government made vaccination compulsory.

Jenner's work was very important. Since 1977 there have been no recorded cases of smallpox. In 1979 the World Health Organisation (WHO) declared smallpox extinct.

> **Revision task**
>
> How did the invention of
> a) the microscope and
> b) vaccination
> improve the treatment of disease?

> **Exam practice**
>
> Describe the work of Edward Jenner in the eighteenth century. **[4 marks]**
>
> **Answers online**

> **Exam tip**
>
> When answering 'describe' questions you need to ensure that you include two to three key factors. To obtain maximum marks you need to support them with specific factual detail, in this instance describing Jenner's experiments with cowpox and how this led to his discovery of the process of vaccination to protect individuals against catching smallpox. You could also mention how he published his research findings in a book called *An Inquiry into the Causes and Effects of the Variolae Vaccinae* (1798).

11.2 What were the main advances made in surgical methods in Britain in the nineteenth century?

During the nineteenth century two major advances improved surgical methods – the discovery of **anaesthetics** and **antiseptics**.

> **Key terms**
>
> **Anaesthetic** – a substance or gas that produces unconsciousness before and during surgery
>
> **Antiseptic** – chemicals used to destroy bacteria and prevent infection in a wound or cut

The development of anaesthetics

Advances in the reputation of surgeons

Revised

Traditionally, surgery was not thought to be a true part of medicine and was not taught in universities. Surgeons watched other surgeons at work and copied them, passing on surgical knowledge. They were most commonly called upon to cut off infected parts of the body or remove kidney stones from the bladder. Surgeons needed to work quickly; they operated with few instruments – a sharp knife and a strong saw. Patients suffered extreme pain and the chances of infection were high.

During the eighteenth century, surgery became more respectable and surgeons began to work in hospitals. This was largely due to the success of several pioneer surgeons.

- William Cheselden (1688–1752) carried out successful operations at St Thomas Hospital, London, and led a campaign for the recognition of surgery as a profession.
- In 1745 the Company of Surgeons was formed; it became the Royal College of Surgeons in 1800.
- William Hunter (1718–83) established a medical school in his house in Windmill Street, London, where he taught surgery; he was helped by his younger brother John Hunter.

- John Hunter is considered to be the 'founder of scientific surgery'; he studied surgery at Chelsea Hospital and St Bartholomew's Hospital in London before becoming a surgeon in the army; in 1768 he was appointed surgeon at St George's Hospital, London, and in 1776 became surgeon to King George III.
- Hunter established his own anatomy school and built up a large collection of human and animal specimens to help with teaching dissection.
- The creation of the Royal College of Surgeons in London in 1800 meant that surgeons had to be registered and properly trained.

The need for anaesthetics – the first experiments

Revised

Several factors hindered advancements in surgery.

- **Pain:** the pain experienced during an operation sometimes resulted in heart failure and death; sometimes patients were hypnotised to avoid pain; alcohol was often used.
- **Speed:** to limit the duration of the pain, surgeons had to act quickly; this hindered accuracy and made mistakes more likely.
- **Infection:** due to the lack of hygiene, wounds often became infected and patients died not from the operation, but from post operative infection.

To overcome these obstacles, several pioneers experimented in the use of substances to limit patients' pain:

- Sir Humphrey Davy (1778–1829) discovered in 1799 that nitrous oxide (laughing gas) reduced pain and he suggested using it during operations.
- Michael Faraday experimented with the liquid ether and found it could relieve pain.
- Robert Liston became the first surgeon in Britain to use ether as a general anaesthetic during an operation in London in 1846.

Ether offered pain-free surgery but its use as an anaesthetic was not without its problems – it irritated the lungs, causing patients to cough during operations; it gave off a nasty smell; and it produced an inflammable vapour. Public opinion was very much against it.

The work of James Simpson

Revised

- James Simpson was Professor of Midwifery at Edinburgh University; he was dissatisfied with using ether as an anaesthetic.
- During 1847 he carried out experiments using different chemicals before discovering the effects of chloroform.
- He started using chloroform to help relieve pain for women during childbirth.
- He wrote articles about his discovery, causing other surgeons to start using chloroform during their operations.

- Chloroform was a new and untested gas; surgeons did not know what dose to give patients. A patient died during an operation in 1848 from an overdose.
- It took Simpson many years to silence his critics over the use of chloroform – its use by Queen Victoria in 1857 as pain relief, during the birth of her eighth child, helped change public opinion.

Chloroform improved surgical techniques by allowing operations to proceed with care rather than speed, and provided effective pain relief for patients.

Revision task

Copy out the table and use information in this section to complete it.

	Sir Humphrey Davy 1778–1829	Robert Liston 1794–1867	James Simpson 1811–70
Name of the anaesthetic pioneered			
The impact of this anaesthetic			

The development of antiseptics

The problem of pain during surgery had been overcome, but the problem of infection remained.

The need for antiseptics
Revised

- Infection was the greatest danger to patients after an operation.
- Surgeons failed to sterilise their equipment.
- Bandages were often reused.
- Some surgeons did not wash their hands before an operation and wore old blood-stained clothes.
- Almost half of all patients who had leg amputations died from blood poisoning.

Joseph Lister and antiseptics
Revised

- Joseph Lister (1827–1912) has been called the 'father of antiseptic surgery'.
- He worked as Professor of Surgery at several universities – Glasgow (1859), Edinburgh (1869) and King's College Hospital, London (1877–93).
- He believed in the 'germ theory' put forward by Pasteur and began experiments to prevent patients from dying from blood poisoning after an operation.
- Lister experimented with using carbolic acid. He washed his hands and all his instruments in it before an operation; soaked bandages in it before applying them to wounds; and soaked silk threads in it before tying up wounds. He reduced the infection rate by doing this.
- He invented a spray machine so that carbolic acid could be sprayed over a patient's wound during an operation.
- He published his findings in 1867; they were met with opposition, especially as Pasteur's germ theory was not yet fully accepted.

Importance and impact of Lister's work
Revised

- Lister's methods marked a turning point in surgery.
- Koch's discovery that a bacterium caused septicaemia (blood poisoning) in 1878 helped the acceptance of Lister's ideas.
- By the 1890s Lister's methods were widely adopted:
  - Operating theatres were thoroughly cleaned.
  - From 1887 all surgical instruments were steam-sterilised.
  - Sterilised rubber gloves were first used in 1894.
- In 1892 Lister, along with Pasteur, was given an award at the Sorbonne University, Paris, in recognition of their contribution to the fight against disease.
- A long-term impact of Lister's work was that the increased ease and safety of surgery stimulated the beginnings of surgical specialisation.

Orthopaedic surgery and Hugh Owen Thomas

Revised

Key term

Orthopaedics – branch of surgery dealing with bone deformities

A member of a family of 'Anglesey bonesetters', Hugh Owen Thomas (1834–91) qualified as a surgeon in 1857 and set up a private hospital in Liverpool. He specialised in **orthopaedics** and developed the 'Thomas Splint', a splint that rested fractured thigh bones and prevented infection. It was used to treat soldiers during the First World War. Thomas became known as *Meddyg Esgryn* ('the bone doctor').

Revision task

List **four** reasons to support the view that Joseph Lister deserves to be regarded as 'the father of antiseptic surgery'.

11.3 What have been the main turning points from the twentieth century to today?

During the nineteenth century, Pasteur and Koch had concentrated on the prevention of disease. During the twentieth century, scientists tried to find 'magic bullets' that could cure illnesses.

Key term

Antibiotics – a group of drugs used to treat infections caused by bacteria

The development of **antibiotics**

The search for 'magic bullets'

Revised

- Paul Ehrlich (1854–1915) was a pioneer of the science of chemotherapy (the use of chemicals to destroy disease-causing organisms).
- Ehrlich and his team experimented with different chemical compounds based on arsenic to find a 'magic bullet' to cure syphilis.
- They experimented with 605 varieties, until they found one that worked in 1905. They named the drug Salvarsan 606. It killed many bacteria including the one that caused syphilis.
- The discovery of Salvarsan was very important – for the first time, a chemical compound had been used to destroy bacteria. This led to further discoveries.
- In 1932 Gerhardt Domagk (1895–1964), a German bacteriologist, discovered that a dye

called Prontosil Red destroyed the bacteria that caused blood poisoning in mice; he tested the drug on humans when his daughter developed severe blood poisoning; she survived and recovered, proving that Prontosil worked.
- The next stage was to discover the active ingredient of Prontosil – this was achieved in 1934 with the discovery of sulphonamide, derived from coal tar.
- Sulphonamides were used to successfully treat puerperal (childbed) fever, scarlet fever, meningitis, pneumonia and gonorrhoea.
- The discovery of these magic bullets were not only important in helping to treat previously incurable diseases, but also in opening up new possibilities for medical cures.

Alexander Fleming and the re-discovery of penicillin

Revised

- John Sanderson first discovered penicillin in the early nineteenth century; in the 1880s Joseph Lister re-discovered Sanderson's work and successfully used penicillin to treat a nurse with an infected wound but Lister left no notes and his research was lost.
- In 1928 Alexander Fleming (1881–1955), Professor of Bacteriology, was working in his laboratory

in St Mary's when he re-discovered *penicillium notatum*, a mould that killed bacteria.
- In 1929 Fleming published a detailed report on the antibiotic powers of penicillin in fighting infection.
- Penicillin quickly came to be seen as an antibacterial 'wonder drug', but it took another ten years to find a means of mass producing it.

Florey, Chain, and the mass production of penicillin

Revised

- Howard Florey (1898–1968) and Ernst Chain (1906–79) were experimental scientists at Oxford University who perfected a method of mass producing penicillin.
- In 1939 they secured funding to set up a team of scientists to research penicillin. By 1941 they had produced enough penicillin to begin human trials.
- The Second World War created a high demand for penicillin to treat infected wounds.
- Due to the war in Europe, Florey took his research to America to secure funding from US drug companies.

- Mass production began in 1943. By the time of D-Day (June 1944), there was enough penicillin to treat all the casualties; by 1945 the US Army was using 2 million doses of penicillin every month.
- At the war's end in 1945, penicillin became available for civilians.
- In 1945 Fleming, Florey and Chain were awarded the Nobel Prize for Medicine for their research into the antibiotic 'wonder drug'.

Revision task

Copy out the table below and use information in this section to complete it.

The discovery and development of four 'magic bullets'		
Name of new magic bullet	Date discovered	Used for treatment of …

Key term

Dialysis – the process of cleaning or purifying the blood of a person whose kidneys are not working properly

Developments in transplant surgery

Early developments in transplant surgery

Revised

The techniques required for transplant surgery were pioneered while treating battle injuries during the Second World War. Sir Archibald McIndoe (1900–60), a Consultant in Plastic Surgery to the RAF, experimented on badly burned fighter pilots, with new techniques in nerve generation, wound healing and tissue reconstruction. His work helped to make the first transplant operations in the 1950s possible.

- The first human organ to be transplanted was the kidney – this took place in the USA in the early 1950s and in the UK in 1960. The kidney was the easiest organ to remove; even if the operation failed, the patient could be kept alive by kidney **dialysis**.

- Work in this field created two immediate problems – rejection of the transplanted organ and the availability of replacement organs.
- There was little progress in heart surgery until the development of a heart-lung machine in 1953; this took over the circulation and oxygenation of the blood, allowing the heartbeat to be stopped so the surgeon had time to work on the inactive heart.
- The 1960s saw the pioneering of heart by-pass surgery. This involved taking veins from the legs to sew into the heart muscle to restore blood supply to the heart muscle (which had suffered from the hardening of the wall of the arteries).

Christiaan Barnard and heart transplants

Revised

- In 1958 Christiaan Barnard started work at the Groote Schuur Hospital in Cape Town, South Africa, and created the hospital's first heart unit. He soon established a reputation as a brilliant surgeon and an expert in the treatment of heart disease.
- In October 1967 Barnard performed the first kidney transplant in South Africa.
- In December 1967 he performed the world's first human heart transplant. The operation on Louis Washkansky lasted nine hours and involved a team of 30 people. The heart transplanted came from a victim of a road fatality, Denise Darvall.

Washkansky survived the operation but lived for only eighteen days, dying of pneumonia.
- Barnard performed a second heart transplant in January 1968; the patient Philip Blaiberg survived for 594 days.
- Barnard performed ten heart transplants between 1967 and 1973, but rejection of the transplanted organ remained a problem.
- Few surgeons copied Barnard until the development of the immunosuppressive agent, cyclosporine, which meant transplants were less likely to be rejected.

Modern transplant surgery

Revised

The pioneering work of Barnard has led to the successful transplant of lungs, liver, pancreas, corneas and even faces.

- By the 1980s many countries had developed nationwide transplant programmes.
- The development of **immunosuppressive drugs** solved the problem of transplant rejection, but not the lack of suitable human organs for transplantation.
- Organ donation remains a controversial issue – the Welsh Government has recently passed legislation to introduce an 'opt-out' rather than an 'opt-in' system of giving consent for organ donation, which will start in 2015. This means that an individual will be assumed to have given consent unless they deliberately opt out of the scheme and carry a card to say so.

Key term

Immunosuppressive drug – a drug that suppresses the body's immune system in order to limit rejection of a transplanted organ

Revision task

Construct a timeline to record the important developments in transplant surgery between 1950 and the present day.

Modern drugs and treatment

Developments in antibiotics, vaccination and public health measures during the twentieth century conquered many killer diseases. Today it is illnesses like cancer and heart disease that are more likely to be the cause of death of most people.

The treatment of cancer

Revised

Cancer is the uncontrolled growth of cells in a part of the human body. Cancerous growths begin because of a change to the DNA of a cell; scientists have not yet found out what causes this change.

- Secondary cancers occur when cancer cells split off and move into vital organs such as the kidneys, the bowels and the lungs.
- The most common cancer among men is lung cancer. A major cause of this is cigarette smoking.
- The most common cancer in women is breast cancer. This used to be dealt with by performing a mastectomy (removing the entire breast), but the more common treatment today is a lumpectomy (removing only the cancerous tumour or lump).

- Scientists are still battling to find cures for the various types of cancer; once cancer has started in the body it can be treated by several processes:
  - **radiotherapy:** attacking the cancer cells with X-rays
  - **chemotherapy:** using chemicals to attack the cancer
  - **surgery:** to remove the cancerous cells by operation
- The fight against cancer includes encouraging prevention by advising regular check-ups, following a healthy lifestyle, and avoiding cancer-causing activities such as smoking.

The treatment of heart disease

Revised

- Heart disease is the most common cause of death in the UK, accounting for one in three deaths.
- Common causes of heart disease are: bad diet, smoking, stress, alcohol abuse, being overweight and viruses.
- Coronary heart disease occurs when the coronary arteries become narrowed by fatty deposits called atheroma which reduces the amount of oxygen-containing blood reaching the heart muscle; this results in pain called angina.
- Part of the atheroma may break off and lead to a blood clot forming; if this clot gets blocked in the coronary artery it can starve the heart muscle of blood and oxygen, causing a heart attack.

- The treatment of heart disease can consist of:
  - ○ advice about diet and exercise
  - ○ use of drugs to steady the pulse, lower blood pressure or reduce cholesterol levels
  - ○ surgery to instal a pacemaker to regulate the heart rate; by-pass surgery; the insertion of a **stent** to widen an artery; heart transplant.

Key term

Stent – short tube of stainless steel mesh

The HIV/AIDS threat

Revised

- In 1981 the first cases of **AIDS** were reported in the USA. In an AIDS sufferer the virus called **HIV** destroys the body's immune system, reducing its defences against attack; the victim does not die of AIDS but of other infections that their body can no longer fight.
- By 2000 an estimated 30 million people were infected with AIDS, the worst affected area being Africa which accounted for 63 per cent of all those infected (19 million); by 2000 over 8 million people had died from AIDS.
- The AIDS virus is spread through the blood or body fluids of infected people – via sexual contact or by sharing injection needles with an infected person.
- Scientists have yet to develop a vaccine or magic bullet that can cure AIDS; the drug Azathioprine (AZT) can prolong the life of an infected sufferer but cannot cure the disease.
- Sufferers have at times been isolated within their communities – e.g. gay men in the 1980s.

Key terms

AIDS – Acquired Immune Deficiency Syndrome

HIV – Human Immunodeficiency Virus

Keyhole and microsurgery

Revised

- In recent years miniaturisation, fibre-optic cables and the use of computers have enabled surgeons to perform keyhole surgery.
- It involves using an **endoscope**, which includes all the tools needed to perform operations on knee joints, hernias, the gall bladder and the kidney.
- Keyhole surgery avoids large incisions and speeds up the recovery process; often patients do not have to stay in hospital overnight.
- Recent advances in microsurgery have enabled surgeons to re-join nerves and small blood vessels, enabling limbs such as fingers and hands to be re-attached after being severed and restoring feeling.

Key term

Endoscope – an instrument used to view the inside of the body

Revision tasks

1. For each of the following diseases write out **two** bullet points explaining how they are currently treated:
   a) cancer,
   b) heart disease and
   c) HIV/AIDS.
2. What is microsurgery?

Exam practice

Have methods of preventing and treating disease always been successful from the Middle Ages to the present day?

[10 marks + 3 marks for SPaG]

Answers online

Exam tip

In this type of 'synoptic' essay you need to focus on the key theme in the question, which in this instance are the words 'always been successful'. You need to cover the period 1345 to the present day, but it is acceptable to divide this up into three or more timeframes.

Chapter 12 Developments in public health and patient care

Key issues

You will need to demonstrate good knowledge and understanding of the key issues of this period:

- How were the sick cared for from the late Middle Ages to 1800?
- What were the main advances in the nineteenth century?
- How has health care improved from the twentieth century to today?

12.1 How were the sick cared for from the late Middle Ages to 1800?

The use of the church and hospitals

Revised

Medieval monasteries played an important role in caring for the sick. The **infirmary** was a type of hospital ward for sick patients. It was separated from the rest of the monastery to stop infection spreading.

In the twelfth century, the Christian Church began setting up hospitals which were run by monks and nuns. They were called 'hospitals' because they offered 'hospitality' by providing shelter to travellers and pilgrims, or a place for the poor and elderly to stay, or a place for **lepers** to shut themselves away. Only a small number of these hospitals actually cared for the sick.

Some medieval hospitals specialised in the type of care they provided:

- St Bartholomew's at Smithfield, London, cared for sick poor people.
- Bethlehem Hospital (often called 'Bedlam') looked after 'lunatics'.
- Christ's Hospital, Newgate, cared for poor fatherless children.

There were no doctors within these hospitals; monks would pray for the souls of the patients while the nuns looked after the welfare of the patients and administered herbal remedies.

Key terms

Infirmary – a hospital or place where sick people are cared for

Leper – a person suffering from leprosy (an infectious bacterial disease which causes scarring and deformities)

The impact of the Black Death

Revised

The Black Death spread across Europe from China during the mid-fourteenth century, killing up to 50 million people. It first entered Britain in July 1348 through the port of Melcombe on the south coast. By the end of 1349 it had spread across England, Wales and Scotland. Up to 40 per cent of the UK population was killed by the disease.

Different types of the Black Death

There were two types of plague and each spread in different ways:

- **Bubonic plague**: this was spread by fleas from black rats; if infected, large swellings called buboes appeared in the armpits and the groin, followed by a high fever and severe headache and the appearance of boils all over the body; death occurred within a few days.
- **Pneumonic plague**: this was spread by people breathing or coughing germs onto one another; the disease attacked the lungs, causing breathing problems and coughing up blood; death occurred quite quickly.

Methods of combating the Black Death

Several methods were used to try to limit the spread of the disease:

- Before entering a town, travellers had to spend up to a month outside the town walls in **quarantine**.
- Infected families were boarded up inside their homes; healthy members were forced to avoid contact with the dying.
- Beggars were paid to take the dead to mass burial pits outside the town walls.
- Some believed the Black Death spread through bad air (miasma – see page 110) and so held scented flowers to their noses; others held their heads over buckets of dung, believing the foul smell would defeat the poison they thought was in the air.
- Some took potions like **theriac**, believing they would kill off the plague.
- Some doctors wore gowns and hoods when making house calls; their hood had a beak which was stuffed with herbs or sponges soaked in vinegar.
- **Flagellants**, believing the disease was a punishment from God, whipped themselves in a display of suffering, hoping the disease would then pass them by.
- Others cleaned their homes, disinfecting the house with herbs; burned brushwood (twigs and small branches) indoors and the clothes of victims, hoping to stop the spread of the infection.

The effects of the Black Death

Medieval people did not understand the link between disease and germs. Towns remained the breeding grounds for infection and vermin and this resulted in further outbreaks of plague after 1348, one of the last being the Great Plague of London in 1665.

The high death toll of the Black Death caused a shortage of labour. Those workers who survived were able to demand higher wages, shorter hours and better working conditions. The Statute of Labourers was issued in 1351 in an attempt to curb wages.

Exam practice

Describe methods of combating the plague during the Black Death. **[4 marks]**

Answers online

Key terms

Quarantine– isolation of a person who may be carrying an infectious disease

Theriac – an ointment or potion used to treat a poison

Flagellant – a person who whips himself as part of a religious penance

Revision tasks

1. Identify **three** functions of a hospital during the Middle Ages.
2. Give **three** reasons to explain why the Black Death spread so quickly.

Exam tip

When answering 'describe' questions you need to ensure that you include two to three key factors. To obtain maximum marks you need to support your points with specific factual detail, in this instance describing the use of potions such as theriac; crouching over dung heaps to kill the foul smell of miasma; the use of scented flowers and herbs; flagellants whipping themselves in the belief the disease was a punishment from God; and the burning of diseased people's clothes.

12.2 What were the main advances in the nineteenth century?

The impact of industrialisation

The growth of industrial towns and cities

Revised

The Industrial Revolution, which began in the mid-eighteenth century, resulted in dramatic changes.

- The growth and spread of factories led to a rapid development of industrial towns and cities such as Glasgow, Manchester, Liverpool, Birmingham, Leeds and Sheffield.
- There was a corresponding sharp rise in population, particularly in the new industrial towns. Manchester and Birmingham saw the largest growth:

Population	1801	1851	1901
Manchester	75,000	303,000	645,000
Birmingham	71,000	223,000	522,000

- The building of new factories also required the building of housing for the workers; rows of terraced back-to-back houses were built next to the factories.
- The lack of any building regulations meant that many were of poor construction and were damp; the streets were unpaved, refuse was not collected and there were no sewers; as a result, drinking water often became contaminated.

Public health problems in industrial towns

Revised

- Poor, squalid living conditions within the new industrial towns meant that outbreaks of disease were common.
- Many **tenement** houses were overcrowded, with large families living in cramped and unhealthy conditions.
- Sewage often found its way into nearby streams and rivers, contaminating drinking water, which led to outbreaks of **cholera**.

Key terms

Tenement – a large building divided into separate flats

Cholera – an acute intestinal infection which causes severe diarrhoea and stomach cramp, caused by contaminated water or food

Outbreaks of cholera and typhoid

Revised

Without proper sanitation and a clean water supply, the filthy conditions in the new industrial towns led to waves of epidemics.

- Cholera first appeared in Britain in October 1831 in Sunderland in north-east England; during 1832 it spread to most towns, causing at least 32,000 deaths; worst hit were the new industrial towns.
- Cholera affected rich and poor alike; germs from the excreta of infected people spread from **privies** into the water supply; in 1832 people did not know infected water spread cholera germs.
- In Wales the years 1832, 1849, 1854 and 1866 saw serious outbreaks of cholera, which caused hundreds of deaths.
- In 1832 Merthyr Tydfil, Wales' largest industrial town, had 160 deaths from cholera; Swansea 152 deaths.
- The 1849 cholera outbreak was more widespread and more deadly.
- **Typhoid** was another killer disease; it was caused by contaminated water or food and spread by bad sanitation or lack of hygiene.

Deaths from cholera, 1849	
Merthyr Tydfil & surrounding area	1682
Cardiff	396
Swansea	262
Neath	245
Newport	209

Key terms

Privies – outside toilets

Typhoid – a serious infectious disease that produces fever and diarrhoea, caused by dirty water or food

Attitudes of the authorities to public health

Revised

For much of the first half of the nineteenth century, local authorities and central government were not interested in public health.

- They adopted a **laissez-faire** attitude, believing it was not their job to interfere in the building of houses, the planning of towns, the collection of refuse or the provision for piped drinking water or sewage disposal.
- They thought that such measures would be expensive to introduce and so claimed it was not their concern.
- The serious outbreaks of cholera in 1832 and 1849 did, however, act as a turning point, causing the government to begin investigating living conditions in the rapidly expanding industrial towns.

> **Key term**
>
> **Laissez-faire** – an attitude that government should not interfere with the way things are run

Revision task

Construct a mind map or spider diagram which identifies the unhealthy living conditions in nineteenth-century industrial towns and cities in Britain.

Public health improvements

The work of Edwin Chadwick

Revised

- Edwin Chadwick (1801–90) was appointed a **Poor Law** Commissioner in 1832; while carrying out his duties he witnessed the dreadful living conditions in the industrial towns.
- He believed in the 'miasma theory' (see page 110).
- He was convinced that there was a link between poor health and bad living conditions. In 1838 he appointed three doctors (Kay, Arnott and Southwood-Smith) to investigate housing conditions in East London.
- In 1839 the government asked Chadwick to head a Royal Commission to enquire into the living conditions of working people.
- In 1842 Chadwick published his findings in his 'Report on the Sanitary Conditions of the Labouring Population of Great Britain'.
- This report highlighted four key findings:
  - ○ Disease killed more people than war.
  - ○ Parliament should pass and enforce laws to make drainage and sanitation effective.
  - ○ These improvements should be funded from local rates and increases in rents.
  - ○ Bad living conditions led to immoral behaviour.
- Chadwick recommended that local authorities should be made responsible for improving drainage, collecting refuse and improving water supplies; he also recommended the appointment of district medical officers to oversee improvements in sanitary conditions.
- Chadwick claimed that such improvements would significantly increase the life expectancy of the labouring classes. His report shocked people but the government was still not quite ready to act.

> **Key term**
>
> **Poor Law** – laws relating to the support of the poor

Victorian health legislation

Revised

In 1843 the government set up a Royal Commission to check Chadwick's findings. It published its 'Report into the Health of Towns' in 1844, having interviewed doctors, Poor Law officials, engineers and architects. The results of this Report were far reaching:

- The Health of Towns Association was set up in 1844.
- A Public Health Act was passed in 1848 which set up a Board of Health run by three commissioners; they had the power to set up local boards of health in areas with high death rates.
- Towns could volunteer to set up their own local health board; 182 towns had done so by 1854.
- The local health boards had the power to:

  - appoint officials
  - make sure that no houses were built without drains or lavatories
  - supply water to households and supervise existing water companies
  - levy a local rate to pay for these improvements.

The cholera epidemic of 1848–49, which killed over 50,000 people, helped to generate interest in public health reform; between 1848 and 1856, 2500 miles (over 4000 km) of new sewer pipes were laid.

However, the Public Health Act of 1848 did not force local authorities to act, it only recommended. Also it had no authority in London. In 1854 the government closed down the Board of Health.

Later Victorian health reforms

Revised

- Cholera returned to Britain in 1854; in the same year, Dr John Snow proved that there was a link between cholera and water supply.
- Dr Snow carried out detailed research into a cholera epidemic centred on Broad Street in Soho, London; he proved that all those infected obtained their water from a single pump; on digging out the pump he discovered that the contents of a nearby cesspit had seeped into the water supply. Snow published his findings in 'On the Mode of Communication of Cholera' (1854).
- Central government now acted and in 1855 appointed Dr John Simon (1816–1904) as Chief Medical Adviser. He helped to push through new legislation.
- In 1858 London experienced the 'Great Stink' and in 1859 Joseph Bazalgette (1819–91) was appointed to oversee the building of London's new sewage system; this dumped the capital's sewage downstream, away from the city.
- Another cholera epidemic in 1865–66 killed 20,000 people; Dr John Simon used this to persuade Parliament to pass a Sanitary Act in 1866, which forced local authorities to construct sewers.

- Simon was also responsible for the Public Health Act of 1875, which made it compulsory for local authorities to lay sewers, drains and pavements; to provide lighting, street-cleaning, fire services; and to appoint a Medical Officer of Health.
- The Artisans' Dwellings Act of 1875 gave councils the power to take over and clear whole slum districts.
- Chadwick's ideas had now been made compulsory; attitudes to public health had moved away from laissez-faire to the government's direct involvement.

Revision tasks

1. What did Edwin Chadwick do to improve public health?
2. Copy and complete this table for years 1848, 1866, 1875:

Year	Act of Parliament	What it did to improve public health

Use Sources A and B and your own knowledge to explain why public health improved in the nineteenth century. **[6 marks]**

Source A: A cellar dwelling in an industrial town in the early nineteenth century

Source B: From a school textbook

'In 1842, Edwin Chadwick wrote a report on the living conditions of working people which drew a link between ill health and the poor conditions in the industrial towns. His work led to the Public Health Act of 1848.'

Answers online

Exam tip

In this type of question you need to identify change and the reasons for that change, making direct reference to the information in both sources linked to your knowledge of this topic area. In this instance you should mention that the poor living conditions shown in Source A existed because industrial towns had been built very quickly with no planning regulations and no sanitary provision. Source B refers to the work of Chadwick, who investigated poor living conditions and in his Report drew a link between ill health and poor living conditions. This helped push the government to pass the Public Health Act in 1848. Chadwick played a major part in bringing about awareness of the need for public health improvement.

Developments in patient care

Following Henry VIII's closure of the monasteries in the sixteenth century, nuns continued the task of nursing patients. The quality of nursing in the hospitals was generally poor. Many nurses lacked any training or medical knowledge, some treated patients with a lack of respect, and some were accused of being dirty. The job was not one for a respectable young lady to perform.

However, during the mid-nineteenth century, three nurses helped to bring about a significant improvement in patient care – Florence Nightingale, Mary Seacole and Betsi Cadwaladr.

The work of Florence Nightingale

Revised

Florence Nightingale (1820–1901) was a pioneer in the way she improved standards in hospitals and patient care.

- She came from a wealthy family and trained as a nurse in Germany and in Paris in 1851–52.
- During the cholera epidemic of 1854 she worked in Middlesex Hospital in London.
- Between 1854 and 1856 Britain fought Russia in the Crimean War; on hearing about the poor treatment of British soldiers in the military hospital at Scutari in the Crimea, Nightingale secured funds from the government to send herself and 38 nurses to Scutari.
- Nightingale could afford to ignore opposition from Army doctors who disliked her interference as she had the support of Sidney Herbert, Minister of War Supplies, and that of *The Times*.

- On arrival at Scutari, Nightingale found that there were 1700 patients in the field hospital, many of whom were suffering from cholera and typhoid, housed in filthy wards.
- One of her first tasks was to clean the wards. Patients were given a regular wash, clean clothes and had their bedding changed regularly. To prevent the spread of disease, patients were separated according to their illness.
- These measures had dramatic results – the death rate in the hospitals fell from 42 per cent to 2 per cent; after just six months only 100 of the 1700 patients were still confined to bed.
- Through these reforms Nightingale laid down new standards of patient care.

The contribution of Mary Seacole (1805–81)

Revised

- Mary Seacole was born in Kingston, Jamaica, the daughter of a Scottish soldier. Her mother ran a medical centre for British soldiers and sailors on the island, where Seacole developed a keen interest in nursing.
- Seacole travelled to London in 1854 and then on to the Crimea to put her nursing skills into

practice; in 1855 she opened the 'British Hospital' between Balaclava and Sebastopol to treat wounded and sick soldiers in the war.

- In 1857 she published an autobiography, *The Wonderful Adventures of Mrs Seacole in Many Lands*, which helped to raise awareness of the contribution of nursing during the Crimean War.

The contribution of Betsi Cadwaladr (1789–1860)

Revised

- Betsi Cadwaladr was born in Bala, north Wales, in 1789, one of sixteen children. Her father was a Methodist preacher.
- Wanting to see the world, she ran away from home aged 14, travelling to Liverpool and then to London. Between 1815 and 1820 she served as a maid to a ship's captain and visited places in South America, Africa and Australia.
- On her return to London she trained as a nurse and in 1854, aged 65, she went to the Crimea to help nurse the wounded soldiers.
- Cadwaladr did not get on well with Florence Nightingale and so moved from the hospital at

Scuteri to Balaclava; she cleaned wounds and changed dressings, working from 6a.m. to 11p.m.

- The war took its toll on her health and she caught cholera and dysentery. She had to leave the Crimea in 1855 and died in 1860.
- The Betsi Cadwaladr **NHS** Trust in north Wales commemorates her.

> **Key term**
>
> **NHS** – National Health Service, which came into existence in 1948 (see page 133).

Hospitals and the development of nursing

- On her return to England in 1856, Florence Nightingale began a campaign to reform army medical services; she called for purpose-built hospitals with trained nurses, clean floors, plenty of light and fresh air, and better food.
- In 1859 Nightingale published her *Notes on Nursing*; *The Times* set up a Florence Nightingale fund, which raised £50,000.
- In 1860 Nightingale used this money to set up training schools for nurses at St Thomas's Hospital and at King's College Hospital in London; the training was based on her principles of patient care.
- When new hospitals were built, such as the Royal Liverpool Infirmary (1887–1889), designers asked Nightingale for advice. Many towns and cities built new hospitals copying this design.
- Some hospitals now began to specialise in types of treatment – hospitals for infectious diseases; for ear, nose and throat issues; eye hospitals – all staffed with trained nurses.
- The basic standards of hospital care had made significant improvements by the end of the nineteenth century. In 1830 there were no trained nurses, by 1900 there were 68,000 and nursing had become recognised as a profession. People were now more willing to go to hospital rather than be treated at home.

> **Revision tasks**
>
> Create a table using the information in this section to explain the contribution made by Florence Nightingale, Mary Seacole and Betsi Cadwaladr to developments in patient care.

12.3 How has health care improved from the twentieth century to today?

Attempts to provide healthier housing and cleaner air

Various attempts were made during the twentieth century to improve housing conditions, the environment and the atmosphere in industrial towns and cities.

The banning of back-to-back housing

- Back-to-back housing was common in nineteenth-century industrial towns, allowing more houses to be packed into a small space.
- The cholera epidemics had discouraged this type of housing.
- Early attempts to improve conditions involved 'cutting through' each pair of back-to-back houses to produce a larger house.
- A more radical solution was to ban any further building of such housing and then to demolish existing housing.
- There was mass demolition of this type of housing in the 1920s, although it continued to exist until the 1960s.

'Homes for heroes'

- By the time of the First World War there was a serious housing shortage and many houses were unfit for people to live in.
- At the end of the war in 1918 the Prime Minister, David Lloyd George, promised to clear away slum housing and replace it with 'homes fit for heroes'.
- The Housing Act of 1919 offered government grants to local councils to build homes for families with low incomes; local authorities also had to carry out surveys of their housing needs and take action to remedy shortages.
- From 1919 to the onset of the Great Depression in the early 1930s, estates of council houses, with gardens, bathrooms and inside lavatories, were built all over the country; they accounted for about a quarter of all housing built in the interwar years, the rest were privately built for owner-occupiers.

Slum clearance

Revised

- In 1933 councils were asked to prepare five-year programmes for the abolition of slum housing; the Second World War intervened.
- The Beveridge Report of 1942 identified 'squalor' as one of the 'Five Evil Giants' facing British society that had to be tackled after the war and could be done by building 'more and better homes'.
- The bombing of British cities during the war resulted in a desperate housing shortage; grants were given to local councils to build new homes and charge low rents; 1.25 million new homes were built by 1951. However, one-third of existing housing in 1951 still had no fixed bath, and 1 million did not have a flush toilet.
- In 1956 government grants to local councils ended, except those for slum clearance.
- During the 1960s many inner-city slums were cleared and replaced by high-rise blocks of flats.

The Clean Air Act, 1956

Revised

- By the mid-twentieth century, the air quality in many industrial towns and cities was heavily polluted.
- Cities like Birmingham and Sheffield had a haze of pollution hanging over them; London experienced frequent bouts of **smog**.
- In December 1952 the 'Great Smog' fell over London; it was so thick it stopped trains, cars and public events. Over 4000 people died of respiratory illness.
- The Great Smog acted as a turning point, causing the government to take action to reduce air pollution.
- The Clean Air Act was passed in 1956 and remained in force until 1964; it introduced smokeless zones in cities; it encouraged the use of cleaner coals, electricity and gas for heating; it tried to relocate power stations away from cities.
- A second Clean Air Act was passed in 1968; by 1971 smoke pollution in Britain's atmosphere had been reduced by 65 per cent.

> **Key term**
>
> **Smog** – a mixture of smoke, fog and chemical fumes which occurs in some busy industrial cities

> **Revision tasks**
>
> 1. What was back-to-back housing?
> 2. How did the First and Second World Wars help to bring about improvements in housing?
> 3. How did the Clean Air Act of 1956 improve air quality?

The establishment of the National Health Service

The need for a National Health Service

Revised

- The Beveridge Report of 1942 identified 'disease' as one of the 'Five Evil Giants' facing British society and suggested that it could be addressed through a free national health service.
- By 1944 the new national health system was being planned, and following the election of a Labour Government in 1945 Aneurin Bevan, Labour MP for Ebbw Vale, was appointed Minister of Health.
- Bevan's first challenge was to convince the public of the need for the creation of a national health service. He argued that everybody had the right to medical treatment according to need; having contributed into a health insurance scheme, everybody should be treated the same, regardless of whether they were rich or poor.

The National Health Service Act 1946

Revised

- Bevan faced opposition to his planned Act from several quarters – many of the authorities and voluntary bodies that ran the 3000 hospitals to be nationalised objected; the British Medical Association (**BMA**) objected, concerned that doctors would become government employees with reduced incomes; it was also argued that the NHS would be very expensive to run.

> **Key term**
>
> **BMA** – British Medical Association, which represents all doctors

- Bevan was able to overcome this opposition. By the time the NHS was created in July 1948 over 90 per cent of doctors had enrolled.
- For a weekly contribution of four shillings and eleven pence (25p), the NHS offered a range of services and care (see diagram below).
- Under the terms of the 1946 Act:
  - hospitals were nationalised and organised into regional health authorities
  - consultants in hospitals received salaries and treatment to patients was free
  - a national system of GPs, dentists and opticians was provided; they received fees according to the number of patients on their registers
  - local authorities were paid to provide vaccinations, maternity care, district nurses, health visitors and ambulances.

Benefits of the NHS

Revised ☐

The demand for health care under the new NHS went well beyond original predictions:

- In 1947 doctors issued 7 million prescriptions per month; by 1951 the figure was 19 million per month.
- By 1949 8.5 million people had received free dental treatment.
- For the first time poorer people now had free access to doctors and medical treatment which previously they could not afford.
- Since its creation, the extent and quality of the treatment offered by the NHS has got better and better; the number of doctors employed had more than doubled by the 1970s; hospitals have been able to carry out more complex operations.
- The NHS has played an important part in prevention as well as cure; it has launched health campaigns to warn of the dangers of smoking, drinking alcohol and the lack of a healthy diet.
- The NHS has had a huge impact on improving the nation's health.

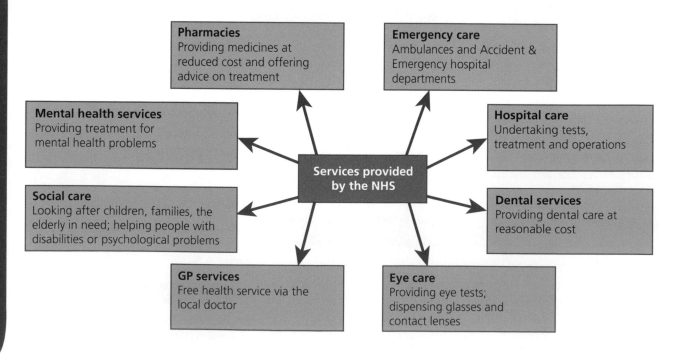

Pharmacies
Providing medicines at reduced cost and offering advice on treatment

Emergency care
Ambulances and Accident & Emergency hospital departments

Mental health services
Providing treatment for mental health problems

Hospital care
Undertaking tests, treatment and operations

Services provided by the NHS

Social care
Looking after children, families, the elderly in need; helping people with disabilities or psychological problems

Dental services
Providing dental care at reasonable cost

GP services
Free health service via the local doctor

Eye care
Providing eye tests; dispensing glasses and contact lenses

Today's concerns regarding health care

To cope with an ever-changing society, the NHS has to constantly evolve and adapt its methods and practices.

Costs of health care

Revised ☐

- The costs of running the NHS have risen sharply and a number of factors account for this:
  - People are living longer due to better medical care
  - Development of new types of drugs to treat diseases such as HIV
  - More complex, expensive operations such as transplants
  - Development of new technology such as scanners
  - Population growth
- In 2007–08 the cost of running the NHS was £44 billion; by 2008–09 this had risen to £48 billion.
- To help pay for this increase some charges have been introduced, e.g. for dental treatment and eye tests.

Greater life expectancy

Revised ☐

- Life expectancy has risen to its highest ever level in the UK.
- A baby boy born in 2009 has a life expectancy of 77.7 years and a baby girl 81.9 years.
- Females continue to live longer than males, but the gap has narrowed.
- In 1948 the gap in life expectancy between male and females was 6 years; by 2009 it had narrowed to 4.2 years.

Ongoing NHS reforms

- In recent years the coalition government has attempted to introduce a radical restructuring of the NHS in England, devolving much of the NHS budget to groups of doctors and introducing more competition into health care.
- The proposal is for Primary Care Trusts to be closed down and the responsibility for health care to be passed on to the groups of GPs who will form General Practice Commissioning Consortiums.
- This is seen as the most radical restructuring of the NHS since its creation in 1948; the debate about these proposed changes is ongoing.

Hospital acquired infections

Hospital cleanliness is a continuing concern due to the appearance of hospital acquired infections. There are currently two major infections causing concern – **MRSA** and **C-Diff**.

- MRSA is a bacterium which is difficult to treat, some strains being resistant to antibiotics. It is an infection which is troublesome for patients with open wounds, those with invasive devices inserted into them or those who have a weakened immune system.
- C-Diff is a bacterium that causes severe diarrhoea and intestinal complaints and in some cases can prove fatal; it can be treated with some antibiotics.
- Since 2004 the NHS has adopted a 'Clean Your Hands' policy and hospital staff, patients and visitors are encouraged to use alcohol-based hand rubs; this policy has reduced instances of hospital acquired infections.

Key terms

MRSA – a bacterium that enters the skin through open wounds to cause septicaemia and is extremely resistant to antibiotics

C-Diff – a bacterium responsible for the majority of hospital acquired cases of diarrhoea in elderly patients

Care in the community

This is the policy of treating and caring for physically and mentally disabled people in their homes, rather than in an institution.

- After much criticism of care institutions, in 1988 the government published its 'Community Care: Agenda for Action' report.
- In 1990 the Community Care Act was passed; the Act came into force in 1993.
- The Act represented the biggest change in mental health care in the history of the NHS, closing asylums for mentally ill patients and integrating those patients into the community.
- There were several reasons for such a policy:
  - Cost effectiveness compared with the previous system
  - The humanitarian and moral rights of the patients
  - To remove the stigma attached to the mentally ill.

Exam practice

Have developments in public health and patient care always improved from the Middle Ages to the present day?

[10 marks + 3 marks for SPaG]

Answers online

Exam tip

In this type of synoptic essay, you need to discuss developments in public health and patient care over a period of time, in this instance examining developments from c.1345 to the present day, making sure you cover the whole period. You should cover at least three timeframes such as the role of the church and hospitals, the contribution of Edwin Chadwick and Florence Nightingale, and the establishment of the National Health Service. Remember to end with a judgement upon the question set.

Revision tasks

1. Explain the pressure placed on the NHS by each factor:
   - Costs of health care
   - Greater life expectancy
   - Hospital acquired infections
2. Explain how the policy of 'Care in the Community' differs from how physically and mentally disabled people were treated in the NHS before 1993.